To our son Jonathan
Mother & Dad.
                    1959.

II Cor. 13:14.
"The favor of the Lord Jesus Christ
" love of God
" partnership of the Holy
Ghost be with you."
                    A.N.T.

Teaching the Word of Truth

BY

DONALD GREY BARNHOUSE

Editor-in-Chief, ETERNITY Magazine

Wm. B. Eerdmans Publishing Company
Grand Rapids, Michigan

PHOTOLITHOPRINTED BY CUSHING - MALLOY, INC.
ANN ARBOR, MICHIGAN, UNITED STATES OF AMERICA

Τῷ ἀγαπῶντι ἡμᾶς καὶ λύσαντι
ἡμᾶς ἐκ τῶν ἁμαρτιῶν ἡμῶν
ἐν τῷ αἵματι αὐτοῦ.

CONTENTS

INTRODUCTION

RATHER than being written, this book grew. In 1927 I became pastor of Tenth Presbyterian Church in Philadelphia, which ever since has been the center of my life work. I discovered that traditional Sunday School methods were inadequate to teach the great doctrines of Scripture. Two devoted women, Mrs. Ruth Tiffany Barnhouse and Miss Elizabeth Haven (now Mrs. Maxwell D. Lathrop), took stories from my sermons, simplified the doctrinal outlines that I was using in Bible classes, and arranged a new course of study for the various departments of our Bible School. Mrs. Barnhouse made all the drawings for the work. We held consultations with the teachers of the Bible School and, on their advice, revised the material; eventually the book was beaten into shape on the anvil of actual practice.

Through the years the Lord has blessed *Teaching the Word of Truth* far more than anyone connected with the work had ever dreamed He would. Tens of thousands of copies have been sold in the United States, and special editions have been published in Great Britain. It has been translated into Arabic, Assamese, French, German, Greek, Japanese, Korean, Congo Swahili, and three languages of India: Hindi, Manipuri and Marathi.

Since its first printing, we have heard actually hundreds of stories of people who have been led to Christ through studying this book—even teachers who used it as a textbook! We cannot tell how many multitudes of young Christians (of any age!) have learned basic doctrine from these simple pages. Surely this illustrates the divine truth of 1 Corinthians 1:28, 29: "God chose what is low and despised in the world, even things that are not, to bring to nothing things that are, so that no human being might boast in the presence of God."

In each of my books the dedication page carries a brief text in Greek. So many people have asked me its meaning that I give its translation: Revelation 1:5*b*: "To him who loves us and has freed us from our sins by his blood."

D. G. B.

HINTS FOR TEACHERS

ONE of the greatest of all Christian works is the teaching of children. We are convinced that much time is spent in teaching them secondary matters while important things—"first things"—are neglected. Of what value is it for a child to know how many miles it is from Jerusalem to Nazareth if he does not know the distance that separates a human heart from God? What is the use of learning the geography of Paul's missionary journeys, or the wanderings of the children of Israel, until he has been taught to bring his own wandering heart to the Saviour?

At every moment the teacher must be conscious of the fact that the children are there and need to be brought to Christ as Saviour and Lord.

Try to make the truth natural to the children. Do not speak in a "pious" fashion, but in a tone of everyday reality. The children should be as free in talking about the Lord as in talking about father or mother. The more you can illustrate from their school and play and homes, the more practical will be the lessons.

Open the lesson with prayer. Often it will be possible to get the children to pray. If a child will pray spontaneously, "Lord bless us as we study Thy Word, and teach us to know Thee," it is more than anything the teacher can say. In small groups children learn to pray aloud without embarrassment.

Each child should have a notebook, and should draw the illustration for himself. This will take only a few moments at the close of the lesson, but that time will be most valuable in fixing the truths taught. Children do not need to be artists to copy these drawings. The "stick men" have been chosen especially because of their simplicity. We have seen good copies of these drawings by five-year-olds. The older children enjoy them more than the younger ones, and will often improve the original drawing. The teacher should insist upon neatness, even where there is little gift of drawing. The Chinese say they do their work well because the gods are looking at them. If this be true of pagans, how much more is it true for us. It is a great lesson to learn that all things may be done "as unto the Lord."

A sense of good comradeship in the class is not hard to develop. A bit of fun is a help, and no teacher need fear to laugh at himself from time to time. The more "human" a teacher is, the greater hold he will have on the class.

It is of extreme importance that the teacher prepare each lesson care-

8

fully. Every verse should be studied and the answers understood. Each teacher is advised to use different translations of the Bible. Read the New Testament passages in Phillips' translation, for example; and all references in both the Revised Standard and King James Versions. Although there are one or two basic errors in the notes of the Scofield Reference edition, it is still the surest means I have found to transform a babe in Christ (of whatever age) into a mature Christian.

The best method of class-room teaching seems to be to question the class first, then explain later. This awakens a wish to know what they cannot answer, and keeps the lesson from seeming dull.

Let the children turn to some verse in the lesson, and explain what it means. Too many older people read the Bible with the idea that they cannot understand it anyway. This training in childhood may keep them from an unintelligent reading of the Bible in later years.

Telling is not teaching. You must find out what your pupils do not know; supply the lack, and then see if they have really understood the teaching you have given.

Try not to use set phrases in teaching your class. If you can talk about the things of the Lord in natural everyday words, instead of the pious words that are so much used in speaking of things spiritual, you have gained much in the understanding of your class.

Each child should have a Bible of his own, and a Bible that can be marked. No Bible is too good to mark. Unhappy the Christian who has a clean Bible after twenty years of the Christian life. Each lesson time an outstanding verse can be underscored. Some like to use colors; red for verses about salvation; black for sin; blue for truths about the Church, the Heavenly people; royal purple for verses about the coming of the Lord, with a line of orange beside a verse that is a golden promise. This is one system that has been used. The teacher may develop others. One child learned to put a figure 3 inside a circle for every verse that spoke of all three persons of the Godhead, and the initials H. S. for every verse that spoke of the Holy Spirit. A cross may be placed in the margin beside verses on the atonement, and a capital R beside verses on the resurrection.

If you have one pupil so bright that he insists on answering all the questions, you may be able to take him into your confidence. Tell him, after class some day, that he is to help you teach. It is to be a secret. He is to watch your eyes, and only answer questions when you look at him. That will give the others a chance to answer first.

Never "talk down" to children. Get on a level with them. If there is anything that children do not like it is reference to their "little hearts" or anything of that kind. They do not understand, either, when you try to tell them what children are like. Treat them as though you were one of them, without being childish in the bad sense.

If a wrong answer is given to a question, instead of saying "no," and giving the correct answer, try stating the question in a different manner. Perhaps you have not made the question clear. If there is a wrong answer, try to give some credit. There is almost always some part of the answer that is right. Take that part and say that it is right, then draw out more truth. Never let the class laugh at anyone's mistakes. If you do you will soon have a silent class.

Remember that children love repetition. The Bible principle is "Precept must be upon precept, precept upon precept; line upon line, line upon line; here a little and there a little" (Isa. 28:10). So you will find that there are many references in later lessons to truths learned in earlier lessons. This must be so with children.

Whenever a Bible verse is referred to, always have the children look it up in their Bibles. This will serve the double purpose of making them familiar with the Bible and of keeping its authority always before them. Never use this volume as authority, and never use your own word as authority. Whenever it is possible, answer a question with, "Let us see what God has to say about that . . ." Then turn to the Bible to get the answer.

A story lives by its details. Wherever possible, take the stories we have given and expand them with the class. Add details that will make them live in the lives and interests of the children.

It goes without saying that some of our lessons are incomplete. We have not given all that the Bible and theology have to say on a given subject. We have given that which will form the elementary background, and upon which the Holy Spirit can build His teaching as the children grow into individual spiritual life.

To draw the crosses, first draw a simple square cross without trying to make the box effect. Then draw the six slanting lines leading from the corners, from left to right. Draw them the same length and at the same angle. Then connect these lines as you see them in the diagram.

GAMES TO BE PLAYED WITH THE CHILDREN

These can be used during opening exercises or after the lesson if there is time remaining.

GAME 1.   VERSE HUNTING DRILL

RULES:

1. All Bibles closed, complete quiet.
2. Announce verse to be found from list you have previously prepared. The lists in our Memory Chart are excellent for this purpose.
3. Tell child not to rise before he has the verse, but to rise and begin reading the moment he is on his feet. This rule avoids the difficulty of children almost having it and starting to rise before they are ready or rising and not yet having the verse.
4. As soon as the verse is read, announce as quickly, "Bibles closed," give a swift glance to see that they are, and announce immediately the next verse. Following these simple rules will make the game proceed rapidly and efficiently.
5. The child who has been first five times is the winner.
6. To encourage the slower ones, announce that only those who have not been first in any of the verses may read the next five ones. Then announce five verses. Let the other ones find them but do not let them read them.
7. The game can be varied using only the New Testament, only the Old or limiting yourself to one book such as the Psalms or Proverbs.

GAME 2.   ENDLESS CHAIN OF NAMES

RULES:

1. The teacher begins or chooses a child to do so, by naming any proper name in the Bible, viz. the name of any person, river, mountain or city. The next child must give a name beginning with the last letter of the preceding name. For example, if Peter is given, the next name must begin with R; if Ruth is then given, the next name must begin with H, etc.
2. Allow one-half minute for the child to think (it is well to have a stop watch) and then pass on to the next. Do not permit the children to speak out of turn or whisper, tell them to keep all they they can think of for their next turn.

11

3. When a child has failed three times he is out. Then he has the
privilege to speak up at anyone's turn if he thinks of a name
beginning with the letter under consideration. Since no name can
be repeated, this brings the game quickly to a close. If the game is
blocked by no one being able to continue, then a new name is given
by the person following the one who was the first to miss that word.

GAME 3. "HANGING"

RULES:

The teacher thinks of a Bible verse and writes blanks on the board
or sheet of paper if the class is around a table, representing every letter
in the verse, marking the separation of words. For example, "Do
all things without murmurings and disputings" (Philippians 2:14),
would be indicated like this: "-- --- ------ -------
---------- --- ----------" (----------- -:--).

As soon as this is on the board, let the children suggest a letter. Have
them raise their hands and let the teacher call on one for an answer.
If the letter is A, put an A in every space where there should be one.
If someone suggested E for this verse there is none, so that letter is
put in the hanging yard. A line of the scaffold is erected with each
wrong letter, and in the end a hanging figure is drawn. If you prefer
to play without using the scaffold, just put the letters in what you
call the "bone-pile."

The child who first guesses the verse and the reference (for this figures
must be suggested) wins the game, and can suggest the next verse.

GAME 4. HIDING

RULES:

The teacher selects a verse anywhere in the Bible. If she selects
Philippians 4:19, she says to the class, "I am hiding in the book of
Philippians, who can find me?" The children open their Bibles
to the book of Philippians. As soon as one thinks he knows where
you are hiding, he puts up his hand. As soon as you say, "All right,
Mary," the child reads the verse he has selected, thus: "You are
hiding in Philippians 1:21. 'For me to live is Christ, and to die is
gain.'" Since this is wrong, you say, "No I am not hiding in Philippians 1:21." The children continue thus until at last one says,
"You are hiding in Philippians 4:19." Then you say, "Yes I am

hiding in Philippians 4:19. Let us all repeat it." Then they all say in concert, "Philippians 4:19. 'But my God shall supply all your need according to his riches in glory by Christ Jesus.'" Do not neglect these continual repetitions, for every repetition of the verses and references has its value in the unconscious mind of the hearers.

Sometimes you can take the most familiar verses throughout the entire Bible, or the New Testament, or just the one book. If you are using our memory system with your group all this verse-training will come much easier.

GAME 5.   TRAPPING GAME

RULES:

1. For the older children who have learned many verses, carry on this game by giving a Bible reference from among the verses they have learned and ask them to quote the verse. This can be done for the smaller ones too, with their more limited number of verses. (See our memory chart.) To vary the game, another time, play it by quoting the verse and asking them to give the reference. Have a stop watch and put a time limit of one minute or even less upon the child who is to answer.

2. Have the children stand in line. Put the first question to the first child. If he misses, it goes to the second and so on until one answers. The child who answers advances in the line to the place of the first one who failed. Do not permit any whispering. If you should overhear anyone doing this, give another verse. Teach the children honesty by demanding that they live it as well as learn verses about it. This can be done gently without giving offence to even the most sensitive. At the close of the game number the children from the foot to the top. When you play it again the foot thus becomes the head. New ones coming in always go to the foot.

3. The same game can be played as a Spelling B using proper names.

1. Gods nature
2. Definition of Sin
3. Mans sin.

LESSON I

SIN:

What It Is

The general idea of sin—"great" sins.

1. The background—God's holiness –Psalm 145:17; Hab. 1:13.
2. What sin is—Matt. 5:8 with Heb. 12:14; 1 John 3:4; 1 John 5:17; Rom. 14:23 b; James 2:10.
3. All are sinners—Rom. 3:23; 3:9; 3:12; 3:19; Jer. 17:9-10.

Object Lesson Illustration: A lightly yellowed and a snowy white handkerchief.

THE rescue mission is an interesting place. There you see men and women dressed in rags, some drunk, some with scarred faces, and some unable to walk. The reason why they are so terrible looking is because of sin. They have gone deep down into sin, and it has left its marks upon them. Just as soon as you look at them you know they are sinners. There are other people who do not look like sinners, beautiful and gracious ladies, men who are kind and generous and who seem to be perfect gentlemen, and do not appear to be sinners like these others; but that is looking at them from the outside only. We cannot see their hearts. Only God can see hearts, and He has told us in His Word secrets about people that we would never guess from looking at the outside.

Here is a handkerchief (the yellowed one). What color is it? White, you say? Now look at this one (the snowy one). The first one does not look so white now, does it? For now you have the whiter one to look at, and the other one seems to be a dirty yellow! That is the way with sin. We speak of little sins and big sins. Some people even talk about "little white lies." That is because they do not realize the holiness of God.

What is holiness? It is perfection—absolute freedom from sin or wrong of any kind. God is perfect. He is holy. Let us find Psalm 145:17 in our Bibles and see what God says about Himself. He says He is righteous in all His ways and holy in all His works. He has never done anything or thought anything that could be even the least little bit wrong. Here is another verse in Habak. 1:13. It says that God cannot look on sin. He

is so pure that when He sees sin, He turns away from it.   When we think of
a holiness like that, all our own goodness begins to look like the dirty
handkerchief when we brought out the very white one.

2.   For God, everything that is not absolutely perfect, is sin.   Here are
some verses that tell us what sin is before God.   (Look up and discuss the
verses under 2.)   Sin is breaking God's law.   God's law is like a measure, and
when the things we do are measured by it, we see how far from perfect they
are.   Just think of the commandment which is called the great commandment of the law.   You will find it in Matt. 22:36-39.   No one has ever kept
it perfectly for one hour!   So you see we have all broken the law, and so
have all sinned, in fact, having broken the first and great commandment,
we are "first and great sinners."

You cannot see into my heart, to see whether or not I am a sinner, and
I cannot see into yours, but God's Word tells.   I know you are a sinner,
and you know I am.   Here are the verses (under 3).   God says we are all
sinners.   That is why Jesus died for us all.

NOTEBOOK SUGGESTION: Explain as the children draw that some people are better than
    others when judged by man's standards, but before God *all* have sinned, and there-
    fore all are under God's condemnation.

B.

LESSON II

SIN:
Its Effects

Always look up the verses in the Bible in order to become familiar with it, and in order to recognize its authority.

Certain causes have definite effects: putting one's hand in the fire causes
   a burn.
1. The ultimate origin of sin and its effect upon the earth—Isa. 14:12-15;
   Ezek. 28:12-19; Gen. 1:2.
2. Sin's effects in individual lives—Ezek. 18:4; James 1:15; John 3:20 b;
   Eph. 2:5; Rom. 6:23.

Lucifer's fall

Lucifer

THERE are some things that never fail to happen. If you put your finger in a flame, you will be burned. This is a law of nature, and never fails to be fulfilled. If you have ever been burned, you know how careful you are afterward to keep away from the fire. You have learned your lesson.

There are some things that never fail to happen in God's working. Just as surely as fire burns, so sin has its results. We are going to see what those results are, and see if we can learn our lesson as well as the lesson about getting burned.

Some people have said, "Did God create Satan? How could God create any one so bad as he?" God's Word shows clearly that God did not create sin or Satan. He created a beautiful angel, high in power and very beautiful, whose name was Lucifer. This angel ruled the universe for God. This angel was perfect in all his ways for a long time. We read about his beauty in Ezek. 28:12-15. But a terrible thing happened, and God tells about it in Isa. 14:12-15. Lucifer stopped looking at God and thinking about Him and instead, looked at himself and began to think about himself. He said to himself, "Why should all the praise go to God? See how beautiful I am! See how great power I have! I will ascend into Heaven. I will exalt my throne above the stars of God; I will be like the Most High." This was the first sin that ever happened, for this was long before God created man. The sin was pride, and because of it, Lucifer was cast down, and lost his power, a great deal of it, and his high place near God. He lost his beautiful name which means "light bearer," and became the Devil.

origin

You see sin is *always* followed by punishment from God.   After Lucifer had sinned God could not let things go on as they were, but had to send Lucifer away from Himself.   That is what sin always does—separates from God.   Another result of Satan's sin is mentioned in Gen. 1:2—"The earth was without form and void."   We know that God did not create it that way.   He made it perfect, but when Satan, the ruler of it all for God, sinned, everything became topsy-turvy.   It became without form and void.

How many years or millions of years passed before God remade the earth, we do not know.   On the sixth day of the re-formation, He made man. You know the story of how man sinned, and how immedi itely, he became afraid of God and hid himself, and as a punishment for his sin, was cast out of the garden.   Again you see that sin brings punishment, and that that punishment is separation from God.   In the Bible, final separation from God is called *death*.   Those who are unbelievers today are far from God and so God says they are dead (Eph. 2:1).   If they never believe, they will be separated from God forever, and this is called the second death.   Those whose souls die in this second death will be far away from God forever and ever.   Here are some Bible verses that speak of this terrible punishment for sin.   (Here the verses under *2* should be found, and discussed.)

NOTEBOOK SUGGESTIONS: Explain that sin makes a high wall between God and men. Since God is holy He cannot have sinful men near Him.   Because men are sinful they cannot come to God.   But when God put sin on the cross (draw in the line to make the cross) then the separation was over and God could come near to men and we can come to Him without fear.   Let each one choose a verse from the lesson to write beneath the cross.   Be sure they write the Bible reference with the verse.

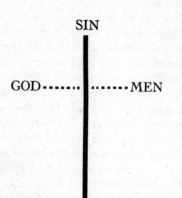

SIN

GOD ······· | ······· MEN

LESSON III

SIN:

Of Believers and Unbelievers

Every object is somewhere; no material thing can be nowhere.
1. The Unbeliever's sins—John 8:24; 1 Tim. 5:24; John 15:22; 9:41.
2. The Believer's sins—Isa 53:6; 2 Cor. 5:21; 1 Pet. 2:24; Heb. 1:3.

Object Lesson Illustration: A book.

IF I take this book in my hand and want to lay it down I cannot lay it nowhere. I must lay it on a table, or a chair, or on the floor, or on something. I cannot just let it drop to nowhere! (As you speak do these different things. Let it drop but call attention to the fact that it lands somewhere.) The same thing is true about sins. They are either on you, or on someone else. You cannot wish them away to nowhere, as perhaps you would like to do.

We know, because God's Word says so, that all are sinners (Rom. 3:23). We know, too, that every sin must be punished, because God is perfectly holy, and so cannot just forget all about sins. But God did not want to separate us from Himself forever. He loved us, even when we were sinners (Rom. 5:8). So He made a way to take our sins from us, and yet be perfectly just. He found a place to put our sins. It was on the Lord Jesus Christ. He was willing to take a human body and a human nature in order to die for our sins.

You remember that when Jesus hung on the cross, there were two thieves crucified with Him, one on either side. At first both of them were cursing and swearing, but after a while one of them became very silent. He knew that he was a sinner, and that he deserved to be punished. He knew too, that Jesus had never sinned, and so he turned to the other thief who was still cursing, and said to him, "Do you not fear God? For we indeed deserve to be punished, but this Man has done nothing wrong." Then he turned to Jesus and said, "Lord, remember me when Thou comest into Thy Kingdom." What he said showed that he truly believed in the Lord Jesus. And Jesus turned to him and said, "Today shalt thou be with me in Paradise." At that moment something happened to the sins of the thief who believed. Until then they had been on himself. He had carried them all his life, but when he believed in Jesus, God took them from him, and put them on Jesus. That was why Jesus was on the cross. He was taking the punishment, not for His own sins (for He did not have any), but for the sins of that thief and of the whole world. The other thief did not believe. His sins remained on him. They could never be put on Jesus. So the unbelieving thief died in his sins.

Which one of those thieves do you want to be like? Let us bow our heads and shut our eyes, and tell God, each one for himself, which one of those thieves we want to be like—the one who believed and was forgiven, or the one who did not believe and carried his own sins, and is still carrying them today.

God says some terrible things about the sins of those who refuse to believe in Jesus. He says they shall die in their sins; that their sins will follow after them; that they have no cloak to cover up their sins; that their sins remain on them. Here are some verses about these terrible things. (Here study the verses under 1.)

Those boys and girls who have believed in the Lord Jesus can be very happy though, for God has taken their sins away. They have been blotted out forever.   (Here study the verses under 2.)

NOTEBOOK SUGGESTIONS: Review the lesson as the pupils draw. Let them choose a verse to write below the drawing. Be sure they write the reference with the verse. See teaching hints for best method of drawing crosses.

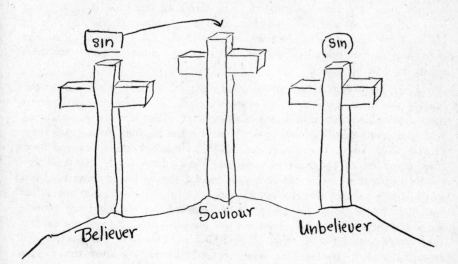

LESSON IV

SIN:

What God Does With Our Sins

What happens to a word erased from the blackboard?

1. What God has done with the Believer's sins—Isa. 43:25; 44:22; Psa. 103:12; Isa. 38:17; Micah 7:19; Col. 2:13; Heb. 10:17.

2. What is the Believer's attitude toward sin because of this?—Rom. 6:1, 2.

Object Lesson Illustration: Chalk, blackboard and eraser.

WE write a word on the blackboard. When we have finished with it, we erase it. What becomes of the word? It disappears, does it not? It vanishes. You can never find it again, for it is gone. God has done a more wonderful thing than that with our sins when we have believed on the Lord Jesus Christ as our Saviour, and have seen that He died for us. He takes our sins away. He removes them from us. When the word is erased from the board, the particles of chalk remain on the eraser or fall down on the tray below the board, so that really the chalk that formed the word is all there. But when God takes away our sins, He takes them so far away that they can never be found again. God wants us to know this. He does not want us to be afraid all the time that someday they will come up and face us again. So He says many things about what He has done with our sins since we have believed. Each thing that He says is to show us that our sins are gone, and that we will never, never see them again, here or hereafter.

First, He says He has blotted them out (Isa. 43:25). That is like erasing the word. Did you ever see a great cloud in the skies, and after a few moments look again and find that *it was gone?* That is what God has done with the *great black cloud* of our sins. He has blotted them out forever (Isa. 44:22). In another place (Psa. 103:12) He says He has removed them from us as far as the East is from the West. How far is that? If you should begin going West out into space and I should begin going East out into space, we might travel a million miles a minute for a million years, but we would never get to the place we had started for, though every minute we would be farther apart. God has put our sins so far away from us that they never can be found again. Again God says that He has put our sins behind His back (Isa. 38:17). Where is God's back? We know that God is everywhere present, that there is "nothing hid from Him." Where then could His back be? This means that He put our sins in a place that cannot be found. He says, too, that He has cast our sins in the depths of the sea. In some places the sea is deep, so deep that no one has been able to measure its depth. Our sins are as far away as that. Then He says He has forgiven them (Col. 2:13), and that He will remember them no more (Heb. 10:17). God knows everything, and the only thing He has ever forgotten is the sins of those who believe that Jesus died for them.

Since God has done all this for us, are we going to go on and sin all we want because we know how wonderfully He forgives? Of course not. A person who truly is born again by believing in Jesus, would never think of such a thing. We love Him because He first loved us, and because of His great kindness we desire to please Him (Rom. 6:1,2).

NOTEBOOK SUGGESTION: The pupils may write either just the reference or the verses in full. Draw the cross first in the center of the sheet.

Sin
Isaiah 44:22

West   Psalm   ✝   East
            103:12
                     -Forgiven-
                       -Forgotten-
                         -Gone-

Micah 7:19

TEST QUESTIONS ON SIN ON PAGE 54.

LESSON V

SALVATION

Telling the truth about bad things.

1 What God says about the unsaved:
Lost—Luke 19:10; John 3:16.
Condemned—John 3:18.
Deeds evil—John 3:19.

Under His wrath—John 3:36.
Children of the Devil—John 8:44.
Full of sin—Mark 7:21-23.
Hate the light—John 3:20.

D ID you ever see a decayed bridge across a stream? Suppose you were standing beside such a bridge when an automobile full of people drove up, and asked you whether the bridge were safe, what would you say? Would you tell them to go across, because you didn't want to say something unpleasant about the bridge? Of course not! That would be dishonest and would make it unsafe for the people. Such a thing would be terrible. Yet some people do not like it because God does not say nice things about them in the Bible. They do not like to hear that they are sinners, lost, condemned, children of the devil. They would rather not hear the truth, even though they need to know it.

It is true that the things God says are not very complimentary. But God must tell the truth. He cannot lie, and He knows that the only way for us to be saved is to know about our sin. So the first thing He tells us when He wants us to know about salvation, is that we are sinners.

We know that everybody is a sinner. We cannot see their hearts, and we may never have seen them do anything wrong, yet we know they are sinners because God says so in Rom. 3:23. But just what does it mean to be a sinner? God tells us that sinners are *lost* (Luke 19:10). They are far away from God and cannot find their way back. He says that unless they believe in the Lord Jesus, they will perish (John 3:16). This means that they will be lost forever—they will be far from God through all eternity. He says that they are *condemned* already. We know that God is love, but it is true too that He is just. He is the Judge, and the Judge must always do right. He does not condemn people just because they are sinners, but because they are sinners who do not believe on His Son Jesus Christ. He is able to forgive all sins except the sin of not accepting the Saviour.

Unsaved people often do kind things. They may give of their money to help the poor. They may spend their lives working for the good of men. These things seem to be good to us, but God does not see them as good.

He says their **deeds** are evil (John 3:19). In another place He says such people cannot please Him (Rom. 8:8). Still again He says that even their plowing is sin (Prov. 21:4). Plowing is not bad in itself, any more than going to school, or washing dishes or running errands, but it is sin when it is done by one who is rejecting Jesus as Saviour. Unbelievers are **under His wrath** (John 3:36).

Then, too, God says unsaved people belong to a bad family. Sometimes you may hear people say that God is the Father of everybody. That is not true. God is the Father of all who believe in the Lord Jesus Christ, but of no one else. Jesus said speaking to the Pharisees, "Ye are of **your father**, the Devil" (John 8:44). It is a terrible thing to have such a father. Sin does not come from without, but from within (Mark 7:21-23).

God says all these things because He wants us to be saved. We must see how terrible it is not to be saved in order to want to have Jesus for our Saviour.

NOTEBOOK SUGGESTIONS: Explain to the pupils as they draw that the only entrance to the way to Heaven is by the cross (faith in the Lord Jesus Christ). After we have gone through the gate, our good deeds please God. Good deeds done on the road away from God do not please Him, nor do they take the one on that road a step nearer God, any more than polishing your car, or giving a poor man a ride would get you to the right city if you had taken the wrong turn somewhere. Let them choose a verse to write beneath the drawing. Be sure they write the reference, too. Draw the cross first.

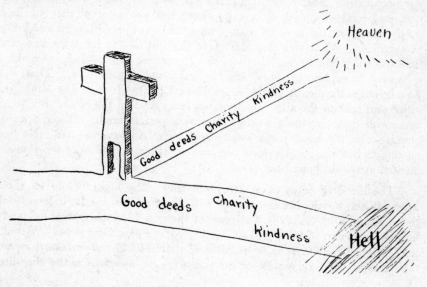

LESSON VI

SALVATION

1. The death of Christ the Way of Salvation—Matt. 26:27, 28; Heb. 9:22.
2. What Salvation is.

THERE was once a problem that God had to solve. Of course nothing is hard for Him because He knows everything. Yet this problem has only one answer. The problem was, how could God save men who are sinners? The reason this is a real problem is because God is holy. He could not just forget about sin. Sin had to be punished. But He could not just punish us all without any mercy, for He is love too. How were God's holiness and love to work together to save men? God found a way— just one way.

All through the Old Testament times He was explaining this way. Do you remember how Cain and Abel brought their sacrifices? Cain brought fruit, and God was displeased with his offering, though it may have been very beautiful. Abel brought a lamb and shed its blood, and though this was not pretty at all, yet God was pleased, and could accept that sacrifice. Again, many, many times we read of how the lambs were brought and killed as sacrifices. What was this for? God did not like to have the innocent lambs killed (Heb. 10:6). That was not the reason at all. God was making a picture, to explain the only way He had found to save men. That way was through the death of the Lord Jesus Christ. Just as the lamb was killed and laid on the altar, so the Lord Jesus died on the cross. The lamb had never done anything wrong. It was a perfect lamb, without spot or blemish. So the Lord Jesus was perfect. He had never sinned. He had no sins to die for. So He took our sins on Himself, and bore the punishment that should have been ours.

The blood of Jesus takes away our sins. The night before He died, when He was having the last supper with the disciples, the Lord Jesus took the cup, and said, "This is the blood of the new testament, shed for many for the remission of sins" (Matt. 26:27, 28). Again God says, "Without shedding of blood there is no remission" (Heb. 9:22). *Remission* means taking away, or forgiveness, or deliverance. So, apart from the shedding of the blood of the Lord Jesus there is no taking away of sin. This taking away of sin is a very important part of salvation.

The Lord Jesus gave His life as a ransom for us (Matt. 20:28). His blood was the price paid for our salvation. Silver and gold could not have paid the price for our redemption. So we read that we are not redeemed with corruptible things like silver and gold, but with the precious blood of Christ as of a lamb without blemish and without spot (1 Pet. 1:18, 19).

The Lord Jesus sometimes speaks of us as His sheep. He said He was the good shepherd, and gave His life for His sheep (John 10: 11, 15).

Here are some verses to look up. Each one tells something different about our salvation, and how the Lord Jesus secured it for us. John 12: 24, 32, 33; 3:14, 15.

This last verse says that the Lord Jesus *must* be lifted up on the cross. That was the answer—the only answer—to God's problem of salvation.

NOTEBOOK SUGGESTION: Let each one choose the verse he wishes to write beneath the picture. Be sure they understand the solution of God's problem.

God's Problem

God's holiness + God's love + Sinners = ✝

Cain's Altar

Abel's Altar

A picture of the cross

LESSON VII

SALVATION

Salvation includes:
1. Forgiveness—Luke 7:48; Eph. 1:7.
2. Regeneration—John 3:5-7; 1 Pet. 1:23.
3. Eternal Life—Heb. 5:9; John 3:16.
4. Sonship—John 1:12; Rom. 8:16; 1 John 3:2.
5. Keeping—John 10:28, 29; 1 Peter 1:5.
6. The Holy Spirit—John 14:17; 1 Cor. 6:19.
7. Glory—John 14:2; John 17:24; Rom. 8:30.

Object Lesson: A kaleidoscope—can be found in many 5 and 10 cent stores.

DID you ever see a kaleidoscope? It is a little instrument into which you look, and see beautiful figures. Then you turn it and the shapes of the figures change. You can never see the same thing in it twice, turn and twist it as you may.

Our salvation is something like the kaleidoscope, for it is different every time you look at it. No matter how long you may be saved, you can never find out all the riches that God has for us in salvation.

The first is *forgiveness.* We know that we have all sinned. God says, "All have sinned." So you see we need forgiveness and that is why the Lord Jesus died on the cross. That was the only way our sins could be forgiven. It is by His blood that we are redeemed (Eph. 1:7). The Lord Jesus saw faith in the heart of a very bad woman, and He forgave all her sins (Luke 7:48). He can forgive ours, too.

Another part of salvation is **regeneration.** That is a long word, but it means to be born again. To Nicodemus, a good man and a wise man, Jesus said, "You must be born again" (John 3:5-7). Everyone needs to be born again—not to become a little baby again—but to receive a new life from God. God cannot do anything with our old sinful life. He does not try to patch it. He gives us a new one.

It would be terrible, wouldn't it, to be saved today, and lost tomorrow? We could never be happy if that were the case. But it is not. When we have been born again by believing in the Lord Jesus Christ, the new life that He gives us is not just life that will last for a day, or a week, or a year, or until we sin again, but life that will last forever, just as long as God is. It is called *eternal life* (Heb. 5:9; John 3:16).

We have learned that those who do not believe in the Lord Jesus Christ have Satan for their father. Those who are saved change their family right away. They become God's *children* (John 1:12; Rom. 8:16; 1 John 3:2).

This means that we do not have to be afraid of God any more. He is our own Father, and He loves us more than we can imagine. We can trust Him to take care of us, and can come to Him with our troubles.

Since God is our Father, He has promised to keep us. He is not going to shut us out of Heaven at last. Satan can never get us back into his family again, for God Himself has promised to keep us safe.

Sometimes we wish that we could have been here when the Lord Jesus was on earth. It would have been wonderful to have seen Him; to have watched Him heal a deaf or a blind man; to have seen Lazarus come out of the grave, or to have been there by the seaside and have eaten some of the food that he made for the five thousand people from the five loaves and two fishes. But there is something more wonderful for us today. When the day was over, the five thousand people had to go home. They could not stay with Jesus for ever. But, so that we would not be lonely, when the Lord Jesus went back to Heaven, He sent *the Holy Spirit* to live in our hearts, if we believe in the Lord Jesus Christ. He is always with us, and He gives us power and joy, and peace, and all good things, and tells us about the Lord Jesus (John 14:17; 1 Cor. 6:19). And there are better things saved up for us in Heaven. There we shall be with the Lord Jesus in the place He has prepared for us (John 14:1, 2). Can you imagine what it will be to see Jesus for the first time? That will be glorious. We shall be with Him for ever and shall share His glory in Heaven (John 17:24; Rom. 8:30).

NOTEBOOK SUGGESTIONS: See if you can get the pupils to name differences between the Kingdom of Darkness and the Kingdom of Light. Let them write their own words if they are correct.

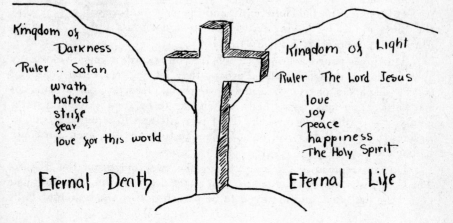

LESSON VIII

SALVATION

Giving and taking.

1. Salvation is by faith.
2. Salvation is not of works.

I KNOW a little girl who is very shy. One day I wanted to give her something, but I couldn't! Over and over I asked her if she would not like it, but she would not stretch out her hand to take it, and finally I had to give up, and the little girl never got the present.

The salvation that we have been talking about in our lessons is God's gift. He wants so much to give it to us, but He cannot unless we will take it. Perhaps that is a little hard to understand. Salvation is not something that you can take in your hand, is it? Our taking is not with our hands, but with our hearts. It is believing what God says about it. This is the way it is. Long ago the Lord Jesus came into the world as a little baby. He was not like other babies, for He was the Son of God. He grew to be a man, and He was always perfect. He never did anything that was even the tiny least bit wrong. But wicked men hated Him and finally they crucified Him. God says in His Word that He died for us. He wants us to believe what He says. If we believe it, He gives us this great gift of salvation, with all its forgiveness, and regeneration, and eternal life, and a new Father, and perfect keeping, and the Holy Spirit, and the glory that we will have is what the Bible means by having faith. (Read and discuss Luke 7:50; 8:48; Mark 9:23; John 3:16; 3:36; 5:24; 6:47.)

Sometimes your teachers in school give you rewards if you are especially good or do your lessons well. Perhaps they let you erase the board, or collect the papers, or give you some other special privilege. Salvation is not a reward. You may try as hard as you like to be good; God can never give you salvation as a reward. That is a gift and it cannot be bought. Besides that, we could never be good enough to deserve it, even if it could be bought.

Do you remember the story about the two thieves on the crosses? The Lord Jesus was being crucified. On either side were thieves. Both had been very bad men, and deserved to be punished. At the beginning both were cursing and swearing. But after a while, one of these thieves became very quiet. The other went on cursing. Finally the one who had been quiet, spoke. He said to the other thief, "Do not you fear God, seeing we are being crucified too? And we ought to be for we have been very bad. But this Man has never done anything wrong." Then he turned to the Lord Jesus and said, "Lord, remember me when Thou comest into Thy kingdom." That man had never done anything to deserve salvation, but the Lord Jesus saw that he believed in Him, and said, "Today shalt thou be with Me in Paradise." He could give him salvation because he believed.

Never try to buy salvation. Going to church; praying, being good, giving money in Church, none of these things can buy salvation for you. It is the gift of God (Rom. 6:23). It is not of works, so no one can be proud of it. God does it all (Eph. 2:8, 9).

NOTEBOOK SUGGESTION: Encourage the pupils to be artistic and neat in their work. Some can do much better than you think.

TEST QUESTIONS ON SALVATION ON PAGE 54.

LESSON IX

THE BELIEVER'S TWO NATURES

Pulling in two directions.
1. The need for the New Nature.
2. What God says about the Old Nature:
    (a) It cannot please God—Ps. 51:5; Eph. 4:22; Rom. 8:8; Jer. 17:9.
    (b) It cannot obey God—Mark 7:21-23; Eph. 2:2.
    (c) It cannot understand God—1 Cor. 2:14; 1 Cor. 1:18; Rom. 3:11.

SOMEONE has drawn a picture of a wagon with a horse hitched to the front and another horse hitched to the back, both pulling as hard as they can. Of course, they cannot get anywhere. In a tug of war you do not go very far—just back and forth. There is a tug of war in the Christian's life, and the only one who can stop it is the Holy Spirit.

Everyone is born with sin in his heart. When a baby is very, very tiny, you cannot see the sin, and the baby does not do anything wrong. But the sin is there, hidden in his heart, and before he gets much bigger it will show forth. We think some people are very bad; others seem to be very good. But God does not see that goodness. He says that all *our* righteousnesses are as filthy rags in His sight (Isa. 64:6). One day there came to Jesus a man who seemed to be very good. He was respectable, for he was a teacher. Probably he was one of the best men in Jerusalem. He came to the Lord Jesus at night, and wished to talk with Him. The very first thing that Jesus said to him was "Verily, verily I say unto thee, Except a man be born again he cannot see the kingdom of God" (John 3:3). All Nicodemus' goodness was not enough. Jesus said he must be born again. Why is this? Why must a person who has never done any thing which seems terrible, be born again? What did Jesus mean?

The answer is this: Everyone is born with an old nature. This old nature is sometimes called "the flesh." That does not mean the flesh of the body, but is the name used for what we are before we believe in the Lord Jesus. This old nature may be educated, and trained so that it does not murder or steal or even lie, but that does not make it good. God says there is nothing good about it. It cannot please Him. Because of this, He wants us to have a new nature that can please Him. That is what He means by being born again. The first time you were born you became alive. But even though your body was alive your soul was dead. When Adam and Eve sinned their souls died, just as God has said—"For in the day that thou eatest thereof thou shalt surely die" (Gen. 2:17). God wants you to be alive, and so He tells you to believe on the Lord Jesus Christ. When you do, He gives you a new life. He does not patch up the old one.

The things that God says about the old nature, the flesh, are not at all pleasant. He had to speak very plainly about it, for if He did not, people would think they could patch up their old nature enough to please God. First He says that the old nature cannot *please* Him. (Discuss the passages under 2a.) Even if one who was not saved should give money to a poor man, the Lord would not be pleased, for it would be the old nature that would be doing it, and as long as one does not believe in the Lord Jesus Christ, nothing that he can do is good.

Then the old nature cannot *obey* God. That is why we cannot save ourselves. (Discuss passages under 2b.)

The old nature cannot *understand* God. Some people say that the Bible seems foolish to them. That is because they do not have the new nature. The *natural* man—that is, the one who has only the old nature cannot understand the Bible, or any of the things about God. If a person says that the cross, and the Lord Jesus dying for our sins seem foolish to them, you can be sure that that is because they have only the old nature. They are perishing (1 Cor. 1:18).

But when we have been born again, we receive the new nature, which can please and obey and understand God. All this God *gives* us when we believe in the Lord Jesus Christ.

NOTEBOOK SUGGESTIONS: Explain that many Christians live according to the old nature and are miserable, when God would have them live happily obeying the new nature instead of the old. This tug of war is described in Gal. 5:17. Following the old nature makes unhappy Christians; following the new makes happy Christians.

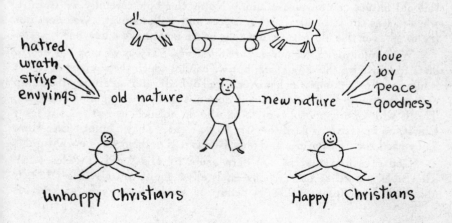

hatred
wrath
strife
envyings — old nature — new nature — love
joy
peace
goodness

unhappy Christians   Happy Christians

LESSON X

THE BELIEVER'S TWO NATURES

The New Nature

The fable of the pig with the deer's heart.
1. The need for the new nature (review of last lesson).
2. How the new nature is received—1 Pet. 1:23; John 1:12, 13.
3. What the new nature is—2 Cor. 5:17; Gal. 2:20; Col. 3:3, 4; Phil. 1: 21; Col. 1:27; 1 John 5:11, 12.

THERE is an old story of a princess who had a little pig for a pet. She kept it in her room with her, and every day it was washed and had a fresh ribbon tied around its neck. She trained it very carefully, trying to teach it to be clean. One day when she had trained it for a long time, she took it out for a walk with her. All went well until they came to a mud hole, when, in spite of his pink ribbon, the little pig jumped right in and began to wallow around, happier than he ever had been before in his life. The princess was very sad, but a good fairy appeared, and told her she would make the little pig love to be clean. She would take away his pig's heart and give him the heart of a deer. A deer is a very clean animal, and so the pig, with his new heart would love to be clean, and would never wallow in the mud again.

Of course, this is only a fable, but it is a picture of what God has to do with us. Like the little pig, we have a heart that loves sin. God says that this old nature cannot please Him. No matter how carefully we train it, when it sees sin, it breaks loose and goes and wallows in it. God does not try to fix over this old nature, but tells us we must have a new one.

We cannot make this new nature ourselves. Try as we may, all we can do is to polish up the old nature, but we cannot touch the sin part of it. It is like painting a pump which is over a well of bad water. Painting the pump makes the pump look better, but it does not make the impure water pure. This is why God cannot accept those who do not believe in the Lord Jesus Christ, no matter how hard they try to do right. They cannot please Him. They need the new nature, and only God can give them this new nature.

God says first that we are born again by His Word (1 Peter 1:23). The Bible is not like other books—it is alive, for it can give life. It tells about the Lord Jesus, and as we believe it, we are born again, and receive

this new nature.   In John 1:12, 13 God tells us how we can become His
children.   We are born again of Him.   It is He who gives us this new life.
When you were born again the Lord Jesus Himself gave you your new life,
just as when you were born the first time, it was your father and mother
who gave you life.   That is why God is the Father of those who believe in
the Lord Jesus Christ.

This new nature is not just patching our old nature.   God only wants
it to die, not to be fixed up.   But the new nature is His life—the Lord Jesus
Himself coming to live in our hearts.   This is why we are called "new crea-
tures" when we are born again (2 Cor. 5:17). Over and over we read that
Christ is our life.   Paul said, "For me to live is Christ."   When we realize
that our new nature is the life of the Lord Jesus in us, we shall want more
and more to let others see Him.

NOTEBOOK SUGGESTIONS: Review the lesson as they draw; try to get the pupils to sug-
    gest their own illustrations; one may say "painting a cup will not change the dirty
    water in it to clean water;" "putting on a pretty frock will not change a girl with
    a mean disposition to a girl with a sweet one," etc. Have them draw what they
    suggest. Select a verse from the lesson to write beneath their picture.

LESSON XI

THE BELIEVER'S TWO NATURES
The Conflict

A caged lion.
1. The old nature is not removed—1 John 1:8, 10; Rom. 7:18; Gal. 5:17.
2. God's provision for victory—Gal. 5:16; Rom. 6:6, 7; Gal. 2:20; Rom. 13:14.

YOU would not like to go to a zoo if all the doors of the cages were opened and the lions and tigers and leopards and hyenas were allowed to go loose. They would immediately begin to fight and kill one another and everything else in sight. But when they are in the cages they can do no harm. They are kept from harming anyone by the iron bars of their cages.

In us we have an old nature that is as bad as a tiger. It cannot do anything good, as we have seen. God will have nothing to do with it. But when we believed in the Lord Jesus Christ and were born again we received a new nature that is all good—and can do nothing wrong, for it is the very life of God which He plants in us. It would be very nice if, when we received the new nature, God should take away the old nature, but He does not. He has a good reason for leaving it in us. Some people have deluded themselves by thinking that the old nature was gone, and have said that they do not sin any more. This is a lie, for God's Word says that we have an old nature and that it can only sin (1 John 1:8, 10). Even Paul had an old nature, all bad (Rom. 7:18). In Gal. 5:17, we read about the struggle of the old nature with the new nature. The old nature (the flesh) desires one thing, and the new nature (the Spirit) desires the opposite. Remember our old example of the wagon with horses pulling in opposite directions. The flesh pulls toward the Devil and the Spirit pulls toward God.

Perhaps you thought when you believed in the Lord Jesus Christ all your struggles would be over, and were disappointed when you found out that you still sinned, and that the Devil still tempted you. The struggle is only begun when you are born again, for until that time you have had only the old nature. Now, you have the new nature to fight with the old.

What is going to happen, then? Are we going to go on sinning all our lives, with the old nature coming out of its cage and sinning every day?

That is not what God wants. He wants us to have the victory over sin. He wants us to honor Him in everything that we do. How can we, though, with this old sin nature in us, ready to sin any moment?

God has made a way for the new nature to have the victory. That is why the Lord Jesus died. He did not die just to save us from going to hell, but to save us from living a life of sin.

When the Lord Jesus Christ died on the cross, God saw all who would ever believe in Him dying there too. So, He says that we are dead with Christ (Rom. 6:8). Even though the old nature is still there, God does not look at it as alive, but as on the cross, crucified with the Lord Jesus. What we must do if we do not want to have this old nature sinning, is to let God really keep it dead. We must yield ourselves to God, and ask Him to keep the old in the place of crucifixion. When we are tempted to sin we can pray to God, "Lord, I know that my old nature has been crucified with Christ, now keep it dead; do not let it get off the cross and begin to sin". God will do it if we will let Him.

Everything we do is done either by the old nature or the new. If we want the new nature to grow, we must feed it the milk of the Word (1 Pet. 2:2), and we must starve the old nature by not giving it the food on which the world grows fat. If we walk in the Spirit, we shall not fulfill the desires of the flesh (Gal. 5:16; Rom. 6:6, 7; Gal. 2:20; Rom. 13:14).

NOTEBOOK SUGGESTIONS: Bring a cardboard heart for the pupils to trace its outline. Have them choose a verse to write beneath the hearts.

LESSON XII

THE BELIEVER'S TWO NATURES
What They Are

The difference between an animal and a man.
1. Body, soul and spirit—1 Thess. 5:23; Heb. 4:12.
2. The new spirit received at the new birth—1 Cor. 2:12.
3. The new soul—2 Cor. 3:18; Gal. 2:20.
4. The new body—Phil. 3:21; 1 John 3:2.

SOME animals are very intelligent indeed. They can learn to do many things. Some dogs are trained to lead blind people safely through the city streets, stopping when they see a red traffic light, and going on when it turns green. It seems as though they know almost as much as men. There is a difference, though, between the most intelligent animal in the world, and the most stupid man, for animals do not worship any God and men always do, whether they worship the true God, or idols. Animals do not worship anything at all.

There are three parts of man, called body, soul and spirit. The body is the only part you can see. It is the part that has the five senses, sight, hearing, smell, taste and touch. Through these senses we know the world around us. If we did not have bodies we would not be able to see, or smell, or hear, or taste or touch. Animals have bodies as we do, with all these five senses. We also have a soul—the part of us that feels, loves and hates. Animals have this too; you know how dogs learn to love their masters, and how they sometimes hate some people. But man also has a spirit—the part of him that knows about God. Animals do not have a spirit—they do not know about God. It is only by the Bible (Heb. 4:12), that we know the difference between soul and spirit.

When we are born, we are born with all these things—body, soul and spirit. All of them are touched by sin—they have to do with the old nature that cannot please God. Our *bodies* get sick and die—this is because of sin. God told Adam that if he disobeyed Him and ate the fruit, he would die. Adam did die, and everyone else has had these troubles with the body because of sin and the sin nature that is in the body. The *soul* is touched by sin too. We hate what we should love and love what we should hate, many, many times. We do not love the Lord with all our heart as we ought to; we love ourselves and our own way better. The *spirit* is touched by sin. It does not know God as it ought to. In Africa and China and India people worship idols, instead of the true God, and even in Britain where we have the Bible, people do not believe in Him, but imagine a God of their own, who is not like the God of the Bible. So all three parts of man are touched by the sin of the old nature, and cannot please God.

When we are born again God begins a work that is going to make new every part of man. The moment we are born again, and receive the new life of Christ, the new nature, we receive a new spirit (1 Cor. 2:12). This new spirit can understand the things of God. The spirit that belongs to the old nature cannot understand these things. That is why you will hear some people who do not believe saying that the Bible is foolish. Of course it is to them, for they do not have the new spirit. But what about the soul? Is God just going to make it over? No; God never patches anything; He always makes everything new. So He begins to make a new soul, a soul that will love His will and hate sin. He does not do all this at once; but day by day, as we let the new nature rule. This will be finished when Jesus comes, for "we know that when He shall appear, we shall be like Him, for we shall see Him as as He is." He is not even going to leave us with this sin-touched body, for when He shall come, even our bodies will be made like His. Then we shall be perfect.

When we die, or when Jesus comes again, we lose our old nature for ever, and at His coming we will have a new body and be perfect in Heaven for ever.

NOTEBOOK SUGGESTIONS: Let the teacher explain that the new spirit is received the moment we believe; the soul is made new day by day as we obey Christ (dotted line to show it is not yet complete); the new body will be received when He comes. Let the pupils choose a verse, or choose one for them, to write under the illustration.

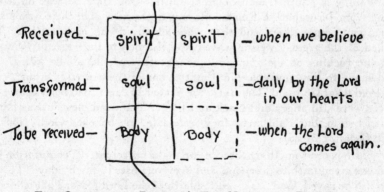

TEST QUESTIONS ON BELIEVER'S TWO NATURES ON PAGE 54.

LESSON XIII

FAITH AND WORKS

Everyday faith.
1. What faith is—Rom. 4:3, 20; Acts 27:21-25.
2. Where faith comes from—Eph. 2:8.
3. The importance of faith—Heb. 11:6.

WE USE our faith every day of our lives. Even people who say they have no faith use it, for it is something we could not get along without. When you drink your milk you have faith that the milk is good and will not make you sick. When you cross a bridge you have faith that it will hold you up. When you ask a policeman the way, you have faith that he knows. When you get into your bed, you have faith that it will hold you up.

Faith is simply believing. Everyone has faith, though not everyone uses it rightly. Abraham was a man of great faith. God gave him certain promises, and Abraham believed them. He had faith. There was nothing to make him believe these promises except that God had done the promising, which is really the greatest reason; but nevertheless Abraham believed. God promised Abraham that he should have a son. Abraham thought that this was impossible, but he did believe God, and God was pleased.

Paul was another man of great faith. One time he was on a ship, going from Jerusalem to Rome. He was a prisoner. On their way a great storm came upon them and they were all afraid—all except Paul. They looked at the great towering waves, and listened to the whistling wind and felt the rocking of the ship and thought they would all be killed. But God spoke to Paul and told him that not one of them would be hurt. Paul believed what God said. The storm was just as bad as it had been before. The waves were still angry and black and high. The wind blew just as hard as it had before, but Paul knew they were safe. He believed God. This was faith (Acts 27:21-25).

Faith is not something that we can make ourselves. It comes from God. God has given faith to everyone, and everyone uses it day by day. To those who will be saved, God has given the faith of the Lord Jesus. That is the kind of faith that saves. The ordinary kind of faith helps people to get along in life; saving faith is the kind that takes us to Heaven. Men cannot believe just by themselves. The Holy Spirit must give them this saving faith. We read in a very wonderful verse, "For by grace are ye saved through faith and that not of yourselves, it is the gift of God" (Eph. 2:8). The grace and the faith and the Lord Jesus in whom we believe are all gifts of God. Everything is from Him.

No one can ever be saved by any other way except by faith. We must *believe* in the Lord Jesus Christ to be saved. Thinking about Him will not do. Praying to Him will not do. Listening to sermons about Him will not do. Reading His Word will not do. All these things are good *after* we have received eternal life, but they will not do a bit of good before. Only believing can save us. Without faith no one can please God. In Heb. 11:6 we read, "For without faith it is impossible to please Him, for he that cometh to God must believe that He is and that He is a rewarder of them that diligently seek Him." No amount of good deeds can please God if they come from a heart that does not believe Him.

God will give saving faith to anyone who will receive it. He wants more than anything else that people shall be saved. Jesus died for your sins on the cross. Do you believe that? Then you have faith, the gift of God, which saves you, and starts you on your way to Heaven.

NOTEBOOK SUGGESTIONS: Tell the pupils that the Bible is full of stories about faith. Ask them for some examples. Then give them their notebooks in which you have copied the sentences below. Have them open their Bibles to the 11th chapter of Hebrews and fill in the spaces with words found there. The words in their order are: creation, sacrifice, translated, ark, obeyed, Isaac, affliction, reproach, Christ, pleasures, Egypt.

By Faith . . We understand . . . .

     Abel offered an excellent . . . .

     Enoch was . . . .

     Noah prepared an . . . .

     Abraham . . . . God.

     Abraham offered up . . . .

     Moses chose to suffer . . . .

     Moses esteemed the . . . . of . . . . greater riches than the

     . . . . of . . . .

Without faith it is impossible to please God.—Heb. 11:6.

LESSON XIV

FAITH AND WORKS

A key to fit the lock.
1. What faith does:
   Saves—Luke 7:50; Rev. 1:5b; Eph. 2:8.
   Justifies—Rom. 5:1.
   Gives everlasting life—John 3:16; 6:47.
2. Works cannot save—Eph. 2:9; Gal. 2:21; Rom. 3:20; Acts 13:39.

IF YOU wish to open a lock, you must have the right key. You may have a whole bunch of keys, but if none of them fit the lock, you might as well have none at all. There is one key, and only one that can open the door of salvation. The name of the key is *Faith*. You may have hundreds of other keys called *Good Works*, but not one of them will open the door.

Faith is just another word for believing. When you believe you are a sinner and cannot save yourself, and that the Lord Jesus died to take your punishment, you have faith, the kind of faith that pleases God. When you have this faith God can take away your sins and give you new life in the Lord Jesus.

The Lord Jesus Himself said that it was faith that saved. A poor sinful woman came to Him one day, and began to wash his feet with her tears, and to wipe them with her hair, and to anoint them with sweet perfume. These surely were good works. But the Lord Jesus spoke to her and said, "Thy faith hath saved thee; go in peace" (Luke 7:50). He did not say, "Thy good works and thy tears have saved thee," but *thy Faith!* Tears can never wash away sin, nor good works cover it up. The Lord Jesus has "loved us and washed us from our sins in His own blood." In another place God says very clearly that "By grace are ye saved through faith, and that not of yourselves, it is the gift of God" (Eph. 2:8).

When we are saved God says we are justified. That means that when He looks at us He does not see any sin, but only the righteousness of the Lord Jesus. Someone has said that "justified" means that it is "just-as-if-I'd never sinned." Of course, God knows we have sinned, but when we have put our faith in the Lord Jesus Christ, He does not see the sin any more. If you look through green glass everything appears green, through blue

glass everything is blue. When God looks at us through the Lord Jesus
He sees us as holy as He sees His Son, Jesus Christ. It is when we believe
what God says about our being sinners, and when we believe what God
says about His being satisfied with the death of His Son that we are saved.
It is faith that justifies us, for God has it written in his word that "Therefore being justified by faith we have peace with God through our Lord
Jesus Christ" (Rom. 5:1).

When we are saved we receive new life from God—everlasting life—
a life that will never, never end. This life is ours by faith, too. You know
John 3:16—"For God so loved the world that He gave His only begotten
Son that whosoever believeth in Him should not perish, but have everlasting life!" It does not say that God gives everlasting life to those who
are good, or to those who pray, or to those who go to church, or to those
who do kind things, though He wants us to do all those things, but He
gives everlasting life to those who believe.

Our own works can never save us. "For by grace are ye saved through
faith and that not of yourselves, it is the gift of God; *not of works* lest
any man should boast" (Eph. 2:8, 9). We cannot be justified by our works
(Rom. 3:20).

NOTEBOOK SUGGESTION: When the pupils have completed their drawing tell them to
write Ephesians 2:8 underneath it. Be sure they understand that God wants good
works, but that we must be saved before we can do anything that will please God.

which
key
fits?

LESSON XV

FAITH AND WORKS

Try to lead the children to Christ as Saviour and Lord.
Reread "Teaching Hints." Even if there has been prayer in the preliminary
exercises, your lesson with your individual group should be opened with
prayer, either by the teacher, or one of the class. You can teach the children to pray very easily in the earlier grades. The first time, put the words
in their mouths. "Jane, will you pray?" Say, "We thank Thee, Lord, for
our Saviour Jesus Christ. Teach us today for His sake, Amen!" Shortly
they will learn to make their own prayer.

Carpenters building a house.
1. The right place for good works—Eph. 2:8-10; Titus 3:8.
2. How to have good works—Phil. 2:13.

IT IS very interesting to watch men build a house. You know how
they begin. First they dig the cellar and lay the foundation. Then
they raise the walls, and finally they put on the roof. If you saw
carpenters building a roof, right on the ground, and when they had it done,
shingles and all, trying to raise it up and to build the walls under it, you
would think you had met some crazy carpenters, and probably you would
be right.

It is just that way with faith and works. Faith lays the foundation.
"For other foundation can no man lay than that is laid, which is Jesus
Christ" (1 Cor. 3:11). On this foundation we are to build with good works.
The verses which you have learned, Eph. 2:8-10 tell us the same thing.
"For by grace are ye saved . . . not of works . . . for we are His
workmanship, created in Christ Jesus *unto* good works." God saved us
so that we would do good works. He has a plan, just as the carpenter has
a blue print, which He made before He made the world, of just the good
works He wanted us to do, even the little ones. He has a plan for this
afternoon, and there are good works in it. Every time you, as a believing
Christian, are obedient and kind you are following His plan. When you
are disobedient or ugly, you are not doing the good works that He had
planned. Titus 3:8 tells us that those who have believed should be careful
to maintain good works. In Romans 8:8 we find out that the good works
that unbelievers do cannot please God. Only those who have believed
can do good works that please Him. You would not buy some knives and
cut the lawn with them, thinking that after they had cut the lawn nicely
they would turn into a lawn mower. Instead you buy a lawn mower, already

made, ready to cut the lawn. Good works cannot make us Christians, but after we are Christians we can do good works.

The reason we cannot do good works before we are saved is that only God can really do good. By ourselves we could never do anything really good. When we are saved He comes to live in our hearts, and then it is really He Who does the good works. In wintertime you wear gloves or mittens. Perhaps you go tobogganing. When you take hold of your toboggan to steer it, what is it that does the steering, your hand or your gloves? Of course, it is your hand. If there were no hand in the glove it could not do anything. So we cannot do anything unless the Lord Jesus lives in us. It is He Who really loves people, in our hearts. <u>He</u> is the One Who is kind, and Who does favors for others. He lives in us, and works in us, "both to will and to do of His good pleasure" (Phil. 2:13).

Peter found this out. Before Jesus died, He told Peter that he would deny Him three times. Peter said, "Oh, no, Lord, maybe all the rest will, but you can count on Peter. I would rather die than deny you." But you know when he was frightened, that he did deny Jesus. But afterwards, when the Holy Spirit came to live in Peter's heart, he was as bold as a lion. He preached about Jesus to the very men who had crucified Him, and told them that they were sinners. He was not afraid to be shut up in prison, and even told his judges that he must obey God, and not them. This was because Christ lived in him, and He did the good works which Peter could not have done himself.

NOTEBOOK SUGGESTIONS: The place of good works in relation to salvation is so commonly misunderstood, that we believe it well to make very sure the pupils understand this simple and very important teaching.

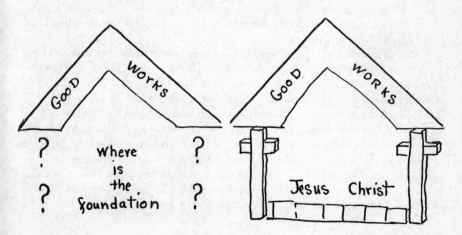

LESSON XVI

FAITH AND WORKS

Try to lead the children to Christ as the Lord and Master of their lives.
How God rewards good works—1 Cor. 3:11-15; Matt. 10:42; 25:21; Rom. 4:4.

THERE is a difference between being paid and being rewarded. If a man works hard all day, he deserves to be paid. If the one for whom he works does not pay him, it is the same as stealing from him, for the wages he has earned are his. Sometimes, though, a kind employer will reward the man who works for him, as well as giving him his pay. Perhaps the man has worked hard all winter long, and has received his pay every week. Then comes summer. The man is supposed to have two weeks' vacation, but his employer says to him, "Well, you have worked very hard and very well, and I am going to give you a month's vacation, instead of only two weeks." That would be a reward. The employer did not have to give it to him, but he did it because he wanted to.

We can never earn wages from God, except the wages of sin. "The wages of sin is death." We all deserved that, for we have all sinned. But you know God paid these wages to the Lord Jesus, when He died on the cross, and so we do not have to receive them. We may try as hard as we like, but we can never earn any other wages from God, for after we have done all that we possible can, we still are imperfect. We cannot earn salvation, and we cannot earn eternal life, and we cannot earn God's blessings. All these things are not wages, and not rewards, but just free gifts, which the Lord gives us freely because He loves us, and because the Lord Jesus Christ has died for us.

But after we have been saved, God does promise us rewards. If we serve Him faithfully, He has some happy surprises saved for us in Heaven. These are rewards. Last week we looked in our Bibles at 1 Cor. 3:11 "For other foundation can no man lay than that is laid, which is Jesus Christ." But look at the next verse, "Now if any man build on this foundation . . ." Any man does not mean any human being, but any believer in Christ, for, of course, a heathen man is not on the foundation, whether he lives in China or in London, or in Chicago. But the way in which a believer builds on the foundation determines the result at the time God gives the rewards. If he does works that are like gold, silver and precious stones, good things that please God, he will receive a reward (v. 14). But if he builds with works like wood, hay, and stubble, worthless works, he will receive no reward. He may be saved himself, but he will have no pleasant surprise when he gets to Heaven. We will all stand before the judgment seat of Christ. If we have believed in Christ, we shall surely go to Heaven, and this judgment is not to see whether or not we can go to Heaven, but to see whether or not we deserve a reward for what we have done after we believed in the Lord Jesus Christ. (Teachers should read the note at 2 Cor. 5:10 in the Scofield Bible.)

Our Lord told a story about a man who had several servants. He was going on a long journey. He called his servants and gave each a large sum of money. To one he gave five talents, to another two, to another one. He told them to use this money for him while he was gone. The man who had the five talents used them well, and before the master came back, he had gained five more. The man who had two talents had gained two more. But the man who had only one was angry and would not use it, and went and hid it in the ground. When the master came back he rewarded the faithful servants, but he was very angry with the servant who had not been faithful, and cast him out into outer darkness.

God has given us salvation and eternal life. He wants us to do what pleases Him. If you are faithful and honest and kind in school and at home, He will reward you. If not, you will lose your reward, and the Lord will not be happy because you have not been faithful.

NOTEBOOK SUGGESTIONS: Explain to the pupils that Christ is the Lord and Master of our lives and that unless we acknowledge Him as such, we are like the servant who hid his talent. We must remember that we are to be faithful in the use of our lives for Him and not to use them for ourselves.

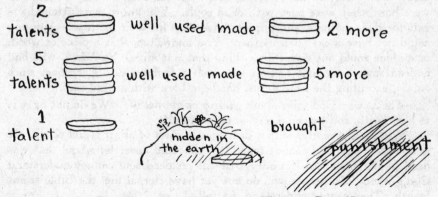

TEST QUESTIONS ON FAITH AND WORKS ON PAGE 55.

LESSON XVII

ETERNAL LIFE

Aim to lead the children to Christ as Saviour and Lord. Have you prayed about your class this week? Bring their particular problems to the Lord and expect to see them solved. Children often understand spiritual things better than adults.

1. What is eternal life?
2. From whence does it come?
3. Why is it needed?

WE ALL know the words "eternal life." We have heard them for many years, but I wonder if we know what they mean. Just what is eternal, or everlasting life? You know what physical life is—it is the opposite of death. A live dog is a dog that is not dead. But the life we are talking about is not just the life of the body, it is the life of the soul. Many of the people whom you see every day have dead souls. Their bodies are alive, but God says they are really dead, "dead in trespasses and sins" (Eph. 2:1); dead while living (1 Tim. 5:6).

But where did this death come from? Surely God did not make Adam and Eve with dead souls? No, that is not correct. Their souls were alive, for Genesis 2:7 says that God made man, and he became a *living* soul. But Adam sinned, and in the moment that he sinned, he died. God had said, "In the day that thou eatest thereof (of the forbidden fruit) thou shalt surely die." He did die—not his body, but his soul. When his children were born, they were born with dead souls. You know that kittens have cats for their mothers, and puppies have dogs for their mothers. A puppy could not have a cat for a mother. You know, too, that a piece of wood, or a stone could not turn into a thing that was alive. So Adam, who had a dead soul, could not have a son with a living soul. Everyone, since Adam, excepting the Lord Jesus, has been born with a dead soul.

This is why God talks about *giving* us eternal life. We do not have it to begin with, and we can receive it only as a gift.

What is the matter with a dead soul? First of all, it is full of sin. It is not holy, and God cannot touch it. He could never let a soul that was dead in sin come into His holy Heaven. A dead soul cannot understand God's Word. To people who do not yet have eternal life, the Bible seems foolish. They cannot understand it at all (1 Cor. 2:14).

God saw these needs, and He provided eternal life for us. Jesus died on the cross, so that God could give us this great gift. "For God so loved the world that He gave His only begotten son, that whosoever believeth in Him should not perish but have *everlasting life.*"

Still we want to know just what this eternal life is. The Bible says that Christ is the life. "Jesus said, I am the way, the truth and the life" (John 14:6). (Look up and read also John 1:4; 1 John 1:2; 1 John 5:13 and 20.) So if you have the Lord Jesus Christ in your heart, you have eternal life.

When Jesus was here He was able to raise the dead (Tell the story of Lazarus—John 11, and Jairus' daughter—Luke 8) because He was the life. He is able also to make dead souls alive, because He is the life. (Read John 11:25; 17:3.) When Jesus is our Saviour, we have eternal life, and our souls are no longer dead. Then we are made holy, and we can also understand God's Word. Philippians 1:21 says that for Paul "to live" was "Christ." He is the only one who can make any of us spiritually alive; and He does it by saving us. That is one reason why He died.

NOTEBOOK SUGGESTIONS: Try to get the pupils to understand that eternity belongs to Heaven and God and that time belongs to earth. Tell them it is hard for us to understand because we can think and talk only in terms of time. Have them write a verse of their choice beneath the illustration.

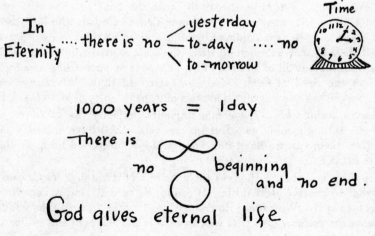

LESSON XVIII

ETERNAL LIFE

Try to lead the pupils to Christ as Saviour and Lord.
Reread "Teaching Hints."
Make out a list of several questions which will be answered in this lesson, and question your class to see if they have really understood what you have taught. If not, you may need to repeat the lesson.

We cannot get eternal life
(a) by what we are,
(b) by what we do.
We must receive eternal life as a gift.

A YOUNG man came to Jesus one day and asked Him what he must do to inherit eternal life (Matt. 19:16-26). He thought Jesus was only a good man, and Jesus had to begin by showing him that He must be called either Good God or bad man. You cannot talk about an honest thief! Then Jesus began to answer his question about life. The great mistake of the young man was to think that life could be received by *doing*. So Jesus answered him, first, by telling him that he had to keep all the commandments, and when the young man said that he had done this, Jesus showed the young man that he had not kept them at all.

If you had a boat tied to the shore by a chain of ten links, which one of the links would you have to cut to cause the boat to go adrift? Any one of the links, you answer. So man was tied to God by the law. Some people break one or two commandments, and think that they keep the rest, but their boat is as much adrift as that of the man who takes a blowtorch and burns out all of the ten links. There is no such thing as a "good sinner" in the sight of God. God has even said that "Whosoever shall keep the whole law and yet offend in one point, he is guilty of all" (Jas. 2:10).

If anyone could keep the commandments perfectly, he could receive eternal life through doing so. But no one can. "All have sinned," God says. How then, can we have this wonderful gift of eternal life? Is there no hope for us?

Yes there is. John 3:16 gives the answer. It is through *believing* in Christ that we receive eternal life. It cannot be earned, simply because we never can earn it. We cannot do enough good works to earn God's favor, because we are sinners. All that we can earn is the wages of sin. "For the wages of sin is *death,* but the gift of God is eternal life, through Jesus Christ our Lord" (Rom. 6:23). Eternal life can only be received as a gift.

Suppose that God said that in order to have eternal life, you must have seven billion dollars. It would be foolish for you to start to save your pennies, hoping to earn that much, for you could never do it. But if a rich friend came along and *gave* you seven billion dollars, then eternal life would be yours. Now God says that we have to keep the commandments perfectly to have eternal life. That is even more impossible than saving seven billion dollars. But the Lord Jesus kept all the commandments perfectly, and if we believe in Him, He gives us His perfect righteousness, and we can have eternal life as a gift. Believe in Him as your own Saviour, and the gift is yours.

When you were born the first time, you received physical life. You began to breathe. You were living. When you are born again, you receive eternal life. Then you begin to live spiritually. Your soul is then alive, not dead in trespasses and sins, as it once was. If you believe that Jesus is the Saviour, you are born again (1 John 5:1).

Anyone who believes will receive this gift of eternal life. It is for "whosoever will" believe. John 3:14, 15, 16 uses this word *whosoever.*

It will be a good plan to have the class look up and mark in their Bibles the following verses: John 3:36; 1 John 5:11; John 5:24; 1 Tim. 1: 15, 16; John 6:40, 47.

NOTEBOOK SUGGESTIONS: When you are sure the pupils have understood the lesson, let them draw the illustration. Perhaps they would like to choose a different verse to write beneath it.

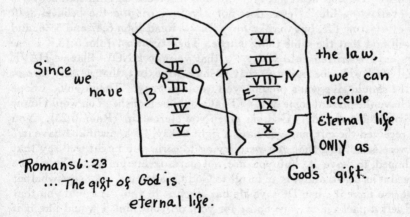

LESSON XIX

ETERNAL LIFE

Assurance That We Possess It

Try to lead the pupils to Christ as Saviour and Lord. If you do not keep ahead of your class in Bible study, you are going to find their questions embarrassing. There are a number of good books on Bible Study that can be had for little outlay.

1. Proof from the Bible that we have eternal life.
2. Proof from experience.
    (a) We believe—John 3:16.
    (b) We love the brethren—1 John 3:14.
    (c) We keep His commandments—1 John 5:2.
    (d) We love God—1 John 5:2.
    (e) We understand God's Word—1 Cor. 2:12.

DO YOU have eternal life? If you ask many people that question, they will answer, "I hope so," or "I expect I will have when I get to Heaven." Such answers show that the people know little about the Bible. You will never find a "hope so" answer in the Bible. Look at John 5:24 "He that heareth My Word and believeth on Him that sent Me hath everlasting life." Jesus does not say that *maybe* the believer *will have* everlasting life, but that he *has* it now. Read John 6:47 and 3:36, and you will find that the same thing is true. Then turn to 1 John 5:13, "These things have I written unto you . . . that ye may KNOW that ye HAVE eternal life." He does not say, that ye may *hope*, but, that ye may *know*.

If I should give you a present, you would not say, "Thank you. I hope I will have the present some day." That would be foolish. You would know that you had it already. God has given you eternal life (Rom. 6:23). You have received the gift, and you have a right to say, "I know that I have it." If it were something that you were trying to earn, you might well say that you hoped to have it, but you are not earning eternal life. You have received it as a gift, and it is an insult to God to say you are not sure whether or not you have it when He says He has given it to you. If I told you that I had left a package at your house for you, do you think I would like it if you said you were not sure whether I had left it or not? Of course not. Surely we must be as polite to God as we are to people. We can always believe His word.

There are a number of other proofs that we have eternal life. Only those who have this eternal life believe. If you believe, you may be sure that you have been born again and have eternal life (1 John 5:1). Those who have eternal life, love other Christians. Read 1 John 5:14. There are some people who are Christians whom you would not like at àll if they were not God's children, because their tastes, and the things they do would not be pleasing to you, but because they belong to God they are your brethren, and you really love them. Those who have eternal life can keep God's commandments 1 John 5:2. If you did not have eternal life, you could not keep even one of God's commandments, for those who have not been born again cannot please God (Rom 8:8). Of course we do not keep His commandments perfectly, but the mere fact that we want to, shows that we have eternal life. Christians, that is, those who have eternal life, love God. Unsaved people do not. They may think they do, and they may talk in a religious sort of way about God, but they cannot love the God who sent His Son to die for us unless they have eternal life. Read 1 John 5:2.

People who do not have eternal life cannot understand the Bible at all. Perhaps you have heard someone say, "I think the Bible is foolish." That does not prove anything against the Bible; it merely shows that the person does not have eternal life. Read 1 Cor. 2:14. If you do not understand French, the language will sound foolish to you. I have seen people laugh and laugh when someone began talking in a language they did not understand. It is the same with the Bible. Until we have eternal life we cannot understand any of it. Now that we are saved, we can understand more every day.

NOTEBOOK SUGGESTIONS: Tell the pupils these are just a few of the "KNOWS" in the Bible and that the Lord does not want us to be ignorant of anything concerning his relationship to us. Draw the center Know first.

Ps. 46:10 Be still and   that I am God.
Ps. 56:9 This I   for God is for me.
Job 19:25 I   that my Redeemer liveth.
If any man will, he shall   the doctrine. John 7:17
 Rom. 8:28 We   that all things work
            together for good.

KNOW

LESSON XX

ETERNAL LIFE

Can Eternal Life Be Lost?

1. God says we are safe.
2. Predestination.
3. The sin question.

SUPPOSE we ask the same question we asked last lesson: Do you have eternal life? Probably you are ready to answer "Yes," now, for God says we may know that we HAVE eternal life, if we believe in the Lord Jesus Christ as our Saviour. But how about tomorrow? Will you have eternal life then? And suppose you should sin, would you lose your eternal life? In other words, our question today is, "Can eternal life be lost?"

If you say eternal life can be lost, you are really saying that eternal life is not eternal. If you had six months life you could lose it at the end of six months. If you had six years life, you could lose it at the end of six years. If you have eternal life you could lose it at the end of eternity, but eternity has no end, so you can never lose it.

But we do not have to guess, for God's Word has something to say about it, very clearly. First of all, Jesus said in so many words that we could never be lost, if we have eternal life. "My sheep hear My voice, and I know them, and they follow Me. And I give unto them eternal life, and they shall never perish, neither shall any man pluck them out of My hand" (John 10:28). So we can never perish. Jesus says so. And he tells us how we are kept—"Kept by the power of God" (1 Pet. 1:5). It was the power of God that made the earth and the sun and the stars. It is by His Power that the earth keeps turning, and that the stars whirl through space and do not collide. It was His power that raised Christ from the dead. So we can be sure that there is no danger of being lost, of our losing our eternal life, for it is the same power that does all these things, that keeps us. Phil. 1:6 says that the One Who has begun a good work in us will keep on perfecting it till Jesus comes. He never leaves His work unfinished, as we sometimes do. If He has begun to save us, He is not going to stop in the middle. Paul was sure of this for he said, "I know Whom I have believed, and am persuaded that He is able to keep that which I have committed unto Him against that day" (1 Tim. 1:12).

One reason why we know that our new, eternal life can never be lost is that God did not make up His mind on the day we believed to save us. We were chosen before He made the world. Read Eph. 1:4. Just think— before there was any man or any earth, God could look down to the present time and see you. And way back there He chose you to be His own. Do you think, after that, that He is going to let you go? Never! Rom. 8:29, 30 tells us that He has predestinated (or planned before) that we should be like Jesus, and that, so far as He is concerned, we are as good as in Heaven, glorified, already.

But what if you sin? What then? The answer is first, that God forgave you once for all for every sin you could commit. When Jesus died, He died for all your sins, not just a part of them. No matter how you might slip, He knew all about it beforehand, even when He chose you. Rom. 5:1 says we are *justified* by faith—it is just as if we had never sinned, so far as God is concerned. He wiped the record clean for us, and we can never be lost. If we sin, He is ready and waiting to cleanse us, and will do it if we confess our sins (1 John 1:8, 9; 2:1). If we refuse to confess to Him, we shall be chastened for our sins (1 Cor. 11:31, 32). But nothing can take away our eternal life, for it is eternal.

NOTEBOOK SUGGESTIONS: Tell the children that it is God's power that keeps the sun, moon and stars in place, and that it is His power that raised the dead. They may suggest other things. Let them draw what they wish and underneath write the verse below, and 1 Peter 1:5.

His power upholds the sun, the moon, the stars.

Hebrews 1:3

He upholdeth ALL things by the word of His power.

His power rolled the stone away

TEST QUESTIONS ON ETERNAL LIFE ON PAGE 55.

TEST QUESTIONS—COURSE ONE

SIN

1. What is sin? What is holiness?

2. How many people in the world have sinned, and how do you know? (Give a verse.)

3. Who committed the very first sin that ever was committed?

4. On whom are the unbeliever's sins?

5. On whom were the believer's sins placed?

6. Was it right for God to forgive one thief and not the other? Why?

7. Tell four things that God says he has done with the believer's sins.

8. Can believers sin all they want, because they know God will forgive?—Why not?

9. What was Lucifer's sin?

10. How can we know our sins have been forgiven?

SALVATION

1. Tell four things that God says about the unsaved.

2. Does it please God if an unsaved man gives money for the missionaries?

3. Was God pleased with the fruit or the lamb in the sacrifices of Cain and Abel? Why?

4. What is the only thing that can take away sin?

5. Do "good" people need to be born again? Why?

6. Do all people have God for their father?

7. Can you save yourself? What is faith?

8. Write Ephesians 2:8-9.

9. What does God give to those who do good works after they are saved?

10. Who is the father of unbelievers?

BELIEVER'S TWO NATURES

1. What is in the heart of all people when they are born?

2. Name three things that God says about the old nature.

3. Can people who have not been born again understand the Bible? Why?

4. Does God make our old nature good?

5. How do we receive the new nature? What is the new nature?

6. What does God want done with the old nature?

7. Are Christians ever tempted to do wrong? Why?

8. How can we have victory over the old nature?

9. What three parts does every man have?

10. Tell when we receive
    (a) The new spirit.
    (b) The new soul.
    (c) The new body.

FAITH AND WORKS

1. What is faith?

2. Can we have faith ourselves, or is it given to us?

3. What saves us, faith or good works?

4. What does it mean to be justified?

5. Who can do good works?

6. Can even a Christian do good work in his own strength?

7. Can we do anything to earn salvation?

8. What wages did we earn by ourselves? Give a verse.

9. What will God give to believers who have done good works?

10. Can good works help to save us?

ETERNAL LIFE

1. Why is everyone born with a dead soul?

2. Was the Lord Jesus born with a dead soul?

3. How can we receive eternal life?

4. What is eternal life?

5. Can we earn eternal life?

6. When does eternal life begin, now or in Heaven?

7. Write John 5:24.

8. Can we ever lose our eternal life? How do you know?

9. When did God choose you to be a Christian?

10. What are we to do when we sin?

COURSE TWO

LESSON I

CHRIST OUR DELIVERER

Try to create an atmosphere of joy in the deliverance of Christ, and love
for Him.

The terrible condition of bondage to sin.
1. Our deliverance:
    (a) Christ's part—the cross.
    (b) Our part—acceptance of Him.

WE HAVE never seen a slave. Long before we were born, about
a hundred years ago, some people who loved the Lord, led by a
man named Wilberforce, had laws passed that bought and set free
all of the slaves in the British Empire. What a time of rejoicing there
must have been when these slaves learned that they were free men and
women!

There are many bad things about slavery. Sometimes slaves had
cruel masters who beat them and treated them very harshly. Some had
kind masters, and these did not object to being slaves. But they all had
the feeling of bondage; they did not belong to themselves, but to their
masters, just as a dog or a cat might belong to you.

We said we had never seen a slave, but that is not quite true. Men
are not slaves to each other in this country today, but many are slaves of
the worst master that ever could be—Satan! Everyone who has ever committed a sin is the servant of sin (John 8:34). This means that every boy
and girl and man and woman is a servant of sin, for we know that "All have
sinned and come short of the glory of God" (Rom. 3:23). Satan is glad to
have many servants, but he hates every one of them, and wishes to do them
all harm. It is a terrible thing to be a slave of sin and of Satan. There is no
real happiness for those who belong to him.

But the worst thing about this slavery is that God has to punish those
who are the servants of sin. He does not hate them as Satan does, but since
He is holy, He must punish sin. Is there any hope for these poor slaves, in
the power of Satan and under the just judgment of God?

Yes, there is! Just as Wilberforce freed the slaves in this country, the
Lord Jesus has signed an emancipation proclamation for all the slaves of
sin and of Satan. They may all go free if they wish to. But the signing
of this proclamation was not like the work of Wilberforce. The Lord Jesus
had to die on the cross in order to be able to free the slaves.

You see, sin is very bad, and since God has to be perfectly fair and just, He cannot forget all about it, but must punish it. So God thought of a way by which sin could be punished without touching the poor slaves of sin whom He loved, even though they were bad. He Himself, in the Lord Jesus Christ, took their punishment for them and let them go free. Now everyone who believes in Him, and takes Him for his Saviour, becomes free from Satan. Christ is our Deliverer.

Let us look at some of the things from which we have been delivered by the Lord Jesus Christ.

Read and discuss the following references: Col. 1:13; 1 Thess. 1:10; Col. 2:13; John 5:24; Matt. 1:21; 2 Cor. 1:10.

NOTEBOOK SUGGESTION: Let the children choose one of the verses to write in full underneath the illustration. Draw the cross first.

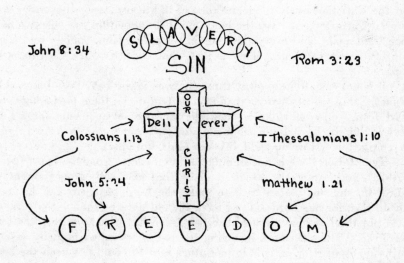

LESSON II

CHRIST OUR DELIVERER

The terrible condition of a sinning Christian.
1. Christ provides deliverance.
    (a) His part—the cross.
    (b) Our part—yielding to Him.

A SLAVE who had been freed would not want to go back to a cruel master who had treated him badly all his life. He would want to keep as far away from such a master as he possibly could. The strange thing about some Christians is that after the Lord Jesus Christ has bought them away from their old master, sin, at such a great and awful price, they seem to want to go back to him and leave the Lord Jesus. That does not seem possible, does it?

It is a terrible thing for a Christian to continue in sin. In Rom. 6:1, 2 we see what God thinks about a Christian's sinning. It is worse for a Christian to sin than for someone who does not belong to God, for the one who belongs to the Devil has all his sins upon him anyway, and one more sin only adds to that terrible list. As a Chinese Christian said, the Devil's people wear dirty clothes anyway, so one more spot doesn't show much, but the Christian wears the white robe of righteousness, so that every spot shows. Then, too, we have the Holy Spirit living within us, when we have been born again, and every time we sin we grieve Him. Surely we do not want to grieve the Lord. That is just what happens when Christians sin (Eph. 4:30).

It is not easy to keep away from sin, even if you have been born again. In fact, Satan will try harder than ever to tempt you then, for he hates our Lord Jesus and would like to steal His servants, even if only for a little while. But the Lord Jesus has made a way so that we never *have* to yield to temptation. If we do yield, it is our fault, not His.

Temptation itself is not sinning. All evil comes from the heart (Mark 7:20-23), and Satan tries to stir it up so that man will caress thoughts of sin, or do the sin. Satan tried to make the Lord Jesus sin, but he could not do this, for our Lord did not have the old nature (John 14:30). So we must not think we have sinned because Satan has tried to stir up the badness in us. The sin comes in loving the evil whether we actually give in to the doing of it or not. Martin Luther said he could not keep the birds from flying around his head, but, by the grace of God he would keep them from building their nests in his hair. God says there is always a way out of temptation for us. Look up 1 Cor. 10:13 and read it. Satan may seem to have blocked every way of escape, but God will show us how to escape, if we ask Him.

The way to let God be our Deliverer from sin and temptation is to go to the cross. You remember it was through the death of the Lord Jesus on the cross that we were saved. He took our punishment for us, and now we are free from sin and the Devil. It is by the cross that we are saved from the punishment of sin, and it is by the cross, too, that we are saved from the *power* of sin. When the Lord Jesus Christ died, God looked at Him and saw Him in our place, so that it was just as if we had really died then, with Him. You know a dead man cannot sin. So when Satan comes with temptation you must say to God, "Father, I know that when Jesus died, I died too. Keep me in the place of death on the cross, so that I will not sin." God will do this if you ask Him. Look up Rom. 6:6 and 11. This is what those verses mean. Our trouble is that too often we like to play with temptation a little while before we ask God to keep us dead to it. And if we do this, before we know it, we will have sinned. So at the very first beginning of temptation, we must yield our hearts to God and ask Him to keep them from sin. Study also 2 Pet. 2:9; Heb. 7:25.

NOTEBOOK SUGGESTIONS: Let the children suggest the temptations they wish to write. Be sure they understand that everyone is tempted and that the Lord wishes us to bring all our temptations to the foot of the cross.

LESSON III

CHRIST OUR DELIVERER

From the Presence of Sin

Point to Christ as the Coming One for Whom we wait.
1. The old nature always present in the Believer.
2. The coming of the Lord to end the old nature.

THERE are some things which we would like to get rid of, but cannot. I have heard of boys who have curly hair, and who do not like it at all. They try in every way to make it lie down straight, but it always curls up again, even if they wish to be rid of it. But things do not leave us just for wishing.

There is something which every Christian has, which he would like to get rid of, but cannot. It is called the "old nature." Every one of us has a life which is bad. It does not like to do right, but always tries to get us to do the things which please Satan and displease our Lord Jesus Christ. These who have not believed in our Lord Jesus have only this life, but those who are saved have a new life besides. The new life is given to us when we believe in the Lord Jesus Christ as our Saviour, and is the very life of God and can never leave us. It is in us, right alongside of the old sinful life. The two never agree. That is why you and I have so many battles to fight in trying to do right. The new nature wants to do right; the old nature wants to do wrong.

There is no way for us to get rid of this old bad life. We may try as hard as we can, but we can never get it to leave us. The Lord Jesus has the power to keep it crucified, dead, as we were saying last week, so that it cannot sin, but even so, it is still there and we must keep yielding ourselves to God all the time, so that it will not pop up and start doing the wrong things all of a sudden. It is like a chained lion. If he were let loose he would do a great deal of harm.

This is not a very pleasant thought, is it? But there is one very happy thing to look forward to. Of course no sin can ever get into Heaven. God has said, "And there shall in no wise enter into it anything that defileth, neither whatsoever worketh abomination or maketh a lie" (Rev. 21:27).

And so, of course, this old nature can never go to Heaven. God tells us that when the Lord Jesus Christ comes back to take us to Himself, the old nature will leave us, and we shall take only the new nature to Heaven. That will last forever, and then we shall have nothing more to do with sin forever and ever. Nothing will ever tempt us then, for there will be no old nature in us to tempt. We shall be like the Lord Jesus Christ—Heb. 9:28; Phil. 3:20, 21; 2 Cor. 5:4, 5; John 17:22; Rom. 8:18, 19.

NOTEBOOK SUGGESTIONS: This simple sketch is excellent for all personal workers. Use it in dealing with adults as well as children. Explain that we should live in the new nature but that many Christians still live according to the old nature; and that most Christians live sometimes in the one, sometimes in the other.

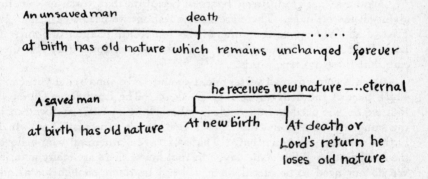

LESSON IV

CHRIST OUR DELIVERER
Section Study on John 14:1-15

Read the passage through *with* the pupils before beginning the lesson.

1. It is from the Word that we must get our knowledge.
2. The three-fold deliverance of the Christian is presented in this chapter.

WE HAVE been talking for the last three lessons about our great Deliverer. Do you remember the three things from which He has delivered us? They are the punishment of sin, the power of sin, and the presence of sin. First, He delivered us from the punishment of sin by taking our place on the cross. Then He delivered us from the power of our old master, Satan, by the fact that when He died, God saw us dead with Christ. Satan is not interested in dead people, especially when they are dead with Christ. And the Lord Jesus is coming again, some day, maybe very soon, to deliver us from the very presence of sin. When He comes, we will have no more old nature in us, to be a traitor and deliver us over to our old master, Satan.

We have just read fifteen verses of Scripture that teach us something about all these things. There are some questions we need to ask ourselves. First of all, Who spoke the words of this fourteenth chapter of John? The Lord Jesus. And He could never make a mistake, could He? So we are sure that these are true words.

We are going to read verses one, two and three, and see if you can tell which part of the deliverance they speak of. The Lord Jesus Christ says that we do not need to be troubled. We believe in God, and we can just the same way believe in Him. He is God, so we can trust Him. In His Father's house—where is that? That is Heaven, where all who believe in the Lord Jesus will live some day. In that house there are many mansions. We do not need to be afraid there will not be room enough for us all in Heaven. Jesus is preparing a place for us and He will come again and receive us to Himself. Can any sin enter into Heaven? Will Jesus take us to Heaven with our old natures in us? Of course not! This part of our chapter is telling us about deliverance from the very presence of sin.

Now look at verse six. This is a verse we should all know. Jesus says He is the only way to God. We cannot go to Him through our prayers or our going to church or our good works. We can only go to God through believing in the Lord Jesus Christ. And when we do come to Him through Christ, what deliverance do we receive? It is the first part of our deliverance—from the punishment of sin. He took that for us, so we can come to God through Him, and be perfectly safe forevermore.

One of the disciples asked a foolish question then. He said He wanted to see the Father. Can we see God today? No. No one can see Him, for He is a Spirit, infinite, eternal and unchangeable. But while the Lord Jesus was on earth, people could see Him. And He was God. So they did not need to ask to see the Father. Jesus told Philip that he should have understood all this, since he had been with Him so long. Then the Lord Jesus went on to talk about His works, and made a wonderful promise. He had done great things, healing the sick and raising the dead. But He promised the disciples that He would give them power so that they could do even greater things. This was to be the power of the Holy Spirit. And it is because of that power that we are not under the dominion of sin. We are freed from its power. So we have all three kinds of deliverance in this chapter.

NOTEBOOK SUGGESTION: Bring a cardboard circle for the children to draw around for the world.

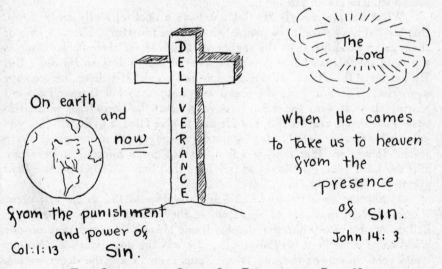

On earth and now

DELIVERANCE

The Lord

When He comes to take us to heaven from the presence of sin.

from the punishment and power of Sin.

Col:1:13

John 14:3

TEST QUESTIONS ON CHRIST OUR DELIVERER ON PAGE 98.

LESSON V

THE SHEPHERD WORK OF CHRIST

Point to Christ, the good Shepherd, Who lays down His life for the sheep.
Shepherds and Sheep.
1. Christ gives His life for us.
2. Christ gives His life to us.

IN THE days when the Lord Jesus lived, there were many flocks of sheep in His country. The shepherds led them to pasture day by day, and took very good care of them. You remember that David the great king of Israel was a shepherd boy. It was not an easy task to be a shepherd, for in those days there were many wild animals, bears, lions and wolves, as well as robbers, who would harm the sheep, and even kill them. A good shepherd would never let anything happen to the sheep. He would rather die first. You remember that David had to kill a bear and a lion, when he was taking care of his sheep.

The Lord Jesus knew that His disciples understood about this work of a shepherd, so one day He said to them, "I am the good Shepherd; and the good Shepherd giveth His life for the sheep."

What did He mean? He did not have a flock of really truly sheep. But He did have sheep; the people who believed in Him. He took care of them more carefully than the shepherds took care of their flock. And as the good shepherds had to guard the lives of their sheep, so He did. But He did more than that. A terrible lion had caught His sheep, before they were His. The lion hurt the sheep and wanted to kill them. He went roaring about looking for sheep to devour. But the Lord Jesus wanted to save those sheep, and He did, but He had to give His life to do it. Can you guess who the lion was? He did not have shaggy mane nor great sharp teeth. It was not that kind of a lion. It was Satan himself: (1 Pet. 5:8). But the Lord Jesus died to set us free from that lion. "The Good Shepherd giveth His life for the sheep."

At another time He spoke of being the door of the sheep. At night the sheep slept in a sort of house where they would be safe. The house had no visible door, but the shepherd was always there, so that no one could come in without his knowing it. He was the door, you see. No one could come in except through Him. Jesus said, "I am the door: by me, if any man enter in, he shall be saved, and shall go in and out and find pasture" (John 10:9).   In another chapter Jesus said, "I am the Way, the Truth and the Life; no man cometh unto the Father but by Me."   He is the only way to God.   It is by believing in Him that we are to be saved, and this is the only way of salvation.

The Lord Jesus not only gave His life *for* us, but He gives His life *to* us.   How can that be?   You see, God says that when we have not yet believed in the Lord Jesus we are *dead;* not our bodies; they are alive, though they too will die some day, but not our souls.   So when Jesus saves us He makes us alive.   And He gives us His very own life.   John 5:24 says, "He that heareth My Word and believeth on Him that sent Me *hath* everlasting life."   In 1 John 5:11 we read, "And this is the record, that God *hath* given to us eternal life, and this life is in His Son."   So you see we already have the life of the Lord Jesus in us, if we have believed in Him, and this life is eternal. The Good Shepherd Who gave His life for us, and gave His life to us, will see to it that His sheep are kept safe from that roaring lion, for He loves them, and cares for them every moment.

NOTEBOOK SUGGESTIONS: Explain that those outside the sheepfold are there because they do not listen to the Shepherd's voice.   Tell again how we must heed the Shepherd's voice and not wander away.   Impress upon them the importance of knowing the Bible, the revelation of the Shepherd's will.   Draw the front wall first.

LESSON VI

THE SHEPHERD WORK OF CHRIST

Point to the Lord Jesus Christ as the risen Saviour Who cares for and keeps
His sheep.
The Good and the Great Shepherd.
1. He is risen from the dead.
2. He keeps His sheep.

THE Good Shepherd died for His sheep. The Lord Jesus died on the cross for our sins. Is He dead now? The answer is in another name of the Lord Jesus. He is not only the Good Shepherd, but the "Great Shepherd," for death could not hold Him. After three days He rose from the dead, and today He is alive, and will be for evermore. There is a verse that tells about this. In Heb. 13:20, 21, we read, "Now the God of peace, that brought again from the dead our Lord Jesus, that Great Shepherd of the sheep, through the blood of the everlasting covenant make you perfect in every good work to do His will, working in you that which is well pleasing in His sight." So you see that though He died, He could not be held by death, but God raised Him for another great work which He was to do for His sheep.

A shepherd might die for his sheep, to save them from a lion, but it would not do to leave them unprotected after that. Another lion might come, or some other danger might threaten. Sheep need to have a shepherd all the time. The Lord knew that people were just like the sheep. We need, not only a Saviour, but a Keeper. So He rose from the dead to do that work.

First of all, the shepherd needs to know every one of his sheep. The Lord Jesus knows each one of His own people. John 10:3 says He "calleth His own sheep by name." He knows your name, and all about you. There is not a thing you do or a thought you think or a wish you have that He does not know all about.

Then He leads His sheep. We do not know what is going to happen tomorrow. It may be a happy day, or it may be a sad day. We may have easy things to do or hard things to do. We need someone to lead us and take care of us, whatever happens. Just as the shepherd leads his sheep to green pastures, and beside still waters, so the Lord Jesus leads us. "The Lord is my shepherd, I shall not want." "When He putteth forth His sheep He goeth before them" (John 10:4). He does not want us to go ahead of Him, but He leads, and all we have to do is to follow Him. In His way there is fulness of joy.

A shepherd might lose some of his sheep. Perhaps a robber chief might come and steal some of them. But there is no robber chief that can steal from the Lord Jesus Christ. He is stronger than anyone. Even the Devil cannot steal us from Him. He said, "My sheep hear My voice, and I know them, and they follow Me, and I give unto them eternal life, and they shall never perish, neither shall anyone pluck them out of My hand" (John 10: 27, 28). Satan may try to take us from Jesus, but he never can, for Jesus is the Great Shepherd, Who rose from the dead, and so showed that He was stronger than Satan. Sin may come, but it cannot take us from Him. He has given His promise that He will keep us, and He will never fail.

NOTEBOOK SUGGESTION: Do not hesitate to assure the children on the authority of the Word of God, the assurance of their salvation; they will do more for love than fear; this is God's way of doing things.

Our Great Shepherd
Hebrews 13:20

We are His people and the sheep of His pasture
Psalm 100:3
They shall never perish. John 10:28

Satan's and Sin's Arrows

LESSON VII

THE SHEPHERD WORK OF CHRIST

Point to the Lord Jesus as the coming One.

The Good Shepherd, the Great Shepherd and the *Chief* Shepherd.
1. The fact of His coming.
2. Our life in view of that fact.

THE Good Shepherd died for His sheep; the Great Shepherd cares for His sheep. Is there anything more that the Lord Jesus, as our Shepherd, can do for us? The Word of God tells us another name for Him, that shows us another great work He is going to do. He is called the *Chief Shepherd.* If you turn in your Bibles to 1 Pet. 5:4, you will read what God has to say about the Chief Shepherd. "And when the Chief Shepherd shall appear, ye shall receive a crown of glory that fadeth not away." The Chief Shepherd is the One who is coming.

We know that God is everywhere at the same time. He is in Heaven, and yet at the same time He is on earth, for He lives in the hearts of all who believe on Him. But now we cannot see our Lord Jesus Christ, though we know He is with us. Yet the day is coming when we shall be able to see Him, for He is coming back to this earth.

The disciples learned about this at the moment when He went away from them into Heaven. They were standing on the Mount of Olives, talking with Him, when He began to ascend into the air, and they watched Him until He disappeared from view among the clouds. Even after He had gone, they stood looking up at the clouds, no doubt wondering if He would appear again. But instead, there stood by them two men, clothed in white, who said to them, Ye men of Galilee, why do you stand looking up into Heaven? This same Jesus, Who is taken away from you into Heaven, shall come again in the same way you have seen Him go.

That is what we are waiting for today. Some day, and it may be soon, the clouds will open, and we shall look up to see the Lord Jesus. He will appear again, and we who believe in Him, shall have our bodies changed, and made perfect, like His glorified body, and shall go up to meet Him in the air and then to Heaven, His home, and ours.

But what is this that the verse says about a crown? The coming Shepherd has been watching over His people, and He is going to reward some of them. This has nothing to do with being saved. Salvation is dependent on believing, and it is never a reward for anything we do. We can never deserve it. But it is a free gift. Yet God is going to reward those who believe, for what they do after they believe. If they let God have His way with them, trusting Him, and obeying Him, they will receive a reward. One of the rewards is for loving His appearing. No one who is living a life of sin, wants Jesus to come back. So if we are truly longing for Him to come, it means that we are living to please Him.

One of the last words we have from the Lord Jesus is in the book of Revelation. It is this: "Behold, I come quickly, and my reward is with me, to reward every man according as his work shall be" (Rev. 22:12).

1 John 3:3 says, "And every man that hath this hope in him purifieth himself, even as He is pure." If we are looking for our Shepherd to come, we will not want to be doing anything displeasing to Him. We will be keeping ourselves pure. If He should come and find us doing anything displeasing to Him, it would spoil for us that great and glorious day of His coming. Let us ask Him to keep us pure.

NOTEBOOK SUGGESTION: Be sure the children realize these are three titles for one Shepherd, Our Lord Jesus Christ.

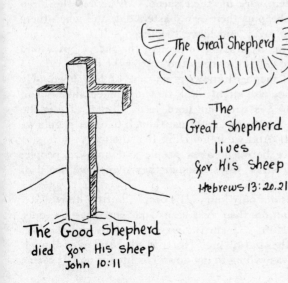

The Great Shepherd

The Chief Shepherd

The Great Shepherd lives for His sheep
Hebrews 13:20.21

The chief Shepherd will come to reward His sheep.
I Peter 5:4

The Good Shepherd died for His sheep
John 10:11

LESSON VIII

THE SHEPHERD WORK OF CHRIST
Section Study of John 10:12-18

Point to the Lord Jesus Christ as the center of our life.
Reread "Teaching Hints."
Read the passage through *with* the pupils.
1. The hireling shepherd.
2. The true shepherd.
3. The death of the shepherd.
4. The fold of sheep.
5. The resurrection of the shepherd.

IT WAS the Lord Jesus Himself Who told His disciples that He was their shepherd. He explained in John 10:1-11 that He was the door of the sheep, and that He would give His life for them, so that all that believed in Him might be saved. Then He went on to tell them more about His shepherd work.

(Let the class read the passage a verse at a time; then discuss as follows):

Verses 12 and 13: Sometimes shepherds had large flocks, and hired under shepherds to help them care for their sheep. Of course the hired shepherds did not love the sheep as their own masters did, and when there was danger, they would run away and leave the sheep. If a wolf came, they would not risk their lives by staying to protect the sheep, but would run away, and the wolf would catch the sheep and scatter the flock.

Verse 14: But the good shepherd knows every one of his sheep. He can tell them apart. Someone else might think they all looked alike but to Him they are different. So it is with our Lord Jesus Christ. He is the Good Shepherd, and He knows every one of us, though to other people we may not be at all important. And we know Him, too, though very imperfectly. That is the difference between saved people and unsaved people. The unsaved do not really know Jesus, though they may have heard of im. We do know Him.

Verse 15: The Lord Jesus not only knows His people, but He knows God the Father. He said that no one had ever seen God, but that the only begotten Son had revealed Him. "I am the way, the truth and the life; no man cometh unto the Father but by me" (John 14:6). And even though He knows the Father, He was willing to lay down His life for us. It seems impossible, does it not? The Lord of Glory, knowing the Father perfectly came down into this sinful world and gave His life for us.

Verse 16: And who are the Lord's sheep? In the days when He was here on earth they were only the Jews. They were the only ones whom He had preached to, and so they were the only ones who had believed. But He did not die only for the Jews, but for the Gentiles, too. He told His disciples that He had other sheep, and that they, too, would be His—one fold, and one shepherd. There are to be no divisions between those who belong to Him. They are all one flock of sheep.

Verse 17: The Father always loved the Son. He said, "This is My beloved Son, in whom I am well pleased." But there was a special reason why He loved the Son in a particular way. It was because the Lord Jesus was willing to lay down His life for the sheep, and because He would be raised from the dead, too.

Verse 18: Some people think that the Jews killed Christ. Others say that our sins made Him die. Both are true, but it was really that He himself willed to die. No one could take His life. He laid it down willingly for us.

NOTEBOOK SUGGESTIONS: When the lesson is taught, tell the children that the Lord wants us to give Him our hearts, to love Him and follow Him, and that to walk away from Him leads to a life of sin and sorrow.

Let us DRAW NEAR with a TRUE HEART
Hebrews 10:22

sin and Sorrow

Joy and peace

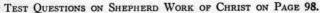

TEST QUESTIONS ON SHEPHERD WORK OF CHRIST ON PAGE 98.

LESSON IX

ACCEPTABLE PRAYER

Point to the Lord Jesus Christ as the One through Whom prayer is possible.

Different kinds of prayer.
1. What is prayer?
2. Who can pray?

IN THIBET everyone prays. But they do not pray as we do. Some have a little prayer written out and put into what looks like a baby's rattle, except that the top part goes round and round as they swing it. They believe that every time the prayer wheel turns the prayer is repeated to their idol. People carry these prayer wheels with them all the time, and keep them turning around all the time. Is this true prayer? Of course not. We know that idols can neither see nor hear nor speak, nor have they any power. They cannot answer prayer. In Old Testament times when a great many of God's people were worshipping the idol Baal, Elijah the prophet gathered all the nation to Mt. Carmel. There the priests of the idol built an altar, and laid a sacrifice on it. Elijah did the same. Then the priests prayed to their idol to send fire to burn the sacrifices. All day long they prayed, but of course there was no answer. Then Elijah prayed, and immediately God answered with fire, and the sacrifice was burned. This showed that God is the true God and that idols are nothing at all.

Prayer is talking to God. It is not just asking for things. When you talk to your mother or father or to your friends you do not just ask for things. You talk about what you are doing and about what they are doing. There are always many things to say to a good friend. Talking to God, or praying, is just like that. We can talk about what we have done all day, and about how good He is, and how loving and kind. We can thank Him for all He has done for us, and of course we can ask Him for what we need, too.

There is a story about two angels who came to earth with baskets to take the prayers of the people to God. One basket was for the "thank-you"s and the other for the "pleases." Which basket do you think was the fuller? It was the "please" basket, for people asked for so many things, and then forgot to say thank you to God. Of course, this is only a story, for God does not have to send angels with baskets to receive our prayers. He hears them Himself. But the story shows us that we often forget to give thanks to God for what He has done for us.

Can everyone pray? No! Some people think that anyone who wants to, can come to God and pray to Him. But that is not true. Not everyone can play on a football team. If you went to the Army and Navy game and asked to be permitted to play on one of the teams, people would just laugh at you. You have to be on the team before you can play. So you have to be in the family of God before you can pray to Him. When we pray we say, "Our Father." You cannot call God your Father unless you are His child and you are His child only if you are saved. "As many as received Him, to them gave He the power to be called the sons of God, even to them that "believe on His name" (John 1:12). If you have believed in the Lord Jesus as your Saviour, you are a child of God, and then you can pray.

When unsaved people pray, they are not praying to God, though they may say His name. They are really praying to Satan, for Satan is the father of all who refuse to believe in the Lord Jesus. When the Pharisees came to Jesus, and said to Him that God was their Father (John 8), He corrected them, and said that their father was Satan.

If we are God's children and hating sin God will hear and answer our prayers.

NOTEBOOK SUGGESTION: Let the children suggest what they wish to write under each column. Help them only when necessary.

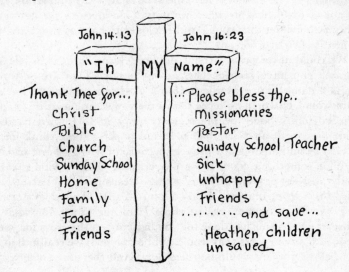

John 14:13 John 16:23

"In MY Name"

Thank Thee for...
Christ
Bible
Church
Sunday School
Home
Family
Food
Friends

...Please bless the..
missionaries
Pastor
Sunday School Teacher
Sick
unhappy
Friends
.... and save...
Heathen children
unsaved

LESSON X

ACCEPTABLE PRAYER

Point to the Lord Jesus Christ as the One through Whose Name we pray.

1. Prayer to the Father.
2. Prayer in the name of the Son.
3. The intercession of the Spirit.

OUR God is not like any other god. The gods of the heathen are idols or demons. Our God is the one Who made Heaven and earth, and Who has been so gracious as to become our Father through the Lord Jesus Christ.

There is only one God. We speak of God the Father, the Son, and the Holy Spirit. This does not mean that we believe in three Gods. He is one God, but He is in three persons. You are only one person, yet you have a body, a soul and a spirit.

When we pray, our prayers have something to do with the three Persons of the Godhead. We pray to God our Father. It is He Who answers our prayers. The Lord Jesus said in John 16:23 that His disciples were to "ask the Father." The Father is not One Who is far away and strange, and Who does not want to hear us when we pray. He loves us far better than any earthly father or mother could, and He loves to hear us pray, and to answer us when it is right to do so.

We could never pray without the Lord Jesus, for it is in His name that we pray. You have seen checks, have you not? They are only good when there is a name signed at the bottom. A checks made out for a hundred dollars would be worth no more than a piece of scrap paper if it had no name at the bottom. Some people seem to pray in their own names. Their prayers are worth no more than pieces of paper. If we think for a minute that God should answer our prayers because of what we are, or because we have done something good, those prayers will go into God's wastebasket. He only answers prayers in Jesus' name. Jesus said, "Whatsoever ye shall ask in *My name*, that will I do" (John 14:13). This does not mean just saying "In Jesus' name" at the end. It means to ask for what you ask, because of what Jesus has done for you in dying on the cross for you. There are a good many prayers that would not be prayed if we really thought about that. Selfish prayers would be ruled out. And there are some prayers that we forget to pray that would be prayed if we remembered about the cross and all Jesus did for us there.

But this is not all there is to prayer. You have seen stools with three legs. They stand very nicely. But if they had only two legs they would fall down. So there is a third part to prayer that makes it stand before God.

We really do not know how to pray. Sometimes we ask for the wrong things. Often we do not pray for the things we should. We do not pray in the right way, so often. But God has made a provision for us. The Holy Spirit, the Third Person of the Godhead, prays with us and for us. Rom. 8:26 tells us that He prays for us for we do not know what to pray for as we ought, but He knows the will of God, and can pray in the right way. So His prayers go to the Father with ours, and God answers in His own good way. Whether the answer is "Yes," "No," or "Wait," we can be sure it is the right answer, and that some day even if we have to wait a long time, we shall understand how very right everything that our Father does, has been for us.

NOTEBOOK SUGGESTION: Emphasize that no one can be heard by God the Father, except he pray through God the Son.

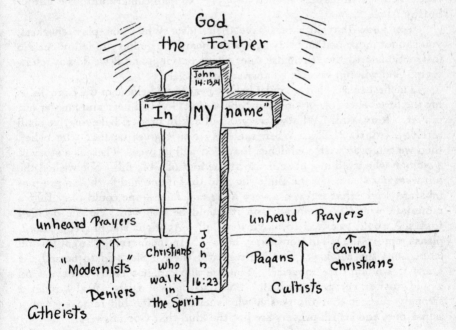

LESSON XI

ACCEPTABLE PRAYER

Point to the Lord Jesus Christ as the One Who makes us able to pray acceptably.
The conditions of acceptable prayer.
Who can pray?

1. Forgiveness of our sins.
2. Faith.
3. Forsaking of iniquity.
4. Forgiveness of others.
5. According to His will.

WE SAID in our lesson last week about prayer, that not everyone can pray. Only those who have believed in the Lord Jesus Christ can pray to God. Jesus said, No one can pray to the Father unless he has had his sins washed away. "No man cometh unto the Father but by Me."

You know that all games have their rules. When you play checkers, you cannot move just any way across the board. You have to follow certain instructions. Just so, there are rules about praying, and if we do not follow them, God will not be able to answer our prayers.

The first rule is that we must believe—not just believe in the Lord Jesus for the forgiveness of our sins, but believe that God will hear and answer our prayer. Jesus said, "Whatsoever ye shall ask in prayer, believing, ye shall receive" (Matt. 21:22). When the Holy Spirit gives us that true belief, then we can pray with confidence that God will answer. There is a story of a woman who lived in a little house at the foot of a big hill. She wished the hill were not there. In the Bible she read that if one had faith as a grain of mustard seed—that is, even a very little real faith—one could pray that a mountain would be removed, and it would be removed. So she decided that she would ask God to move that hill. At night she prayed, "Lord, please remove the hill in front of my house." In the morning she got up and looked out the window. The hill was still there. She said to herself, "I knew it wouldn't be moved!" You see she did not really believe God would answer her prayer at all. She had no real faith. And besides I strongly suspect that the reason why she wanted the hill removed was a selfish one, and selfish prayers are not the kind that God answers.

In Psa. 66:18 we read, "If I regard iniquity in my heart, the Lord will not hear me." If we are holding on to some sin, loving it, and keeping it in our hearts, our prayers cannot be answered. If we confess our sins to Him, He will forgive us our sins, and then He will be able to hear our prayers.

"And when ye stand praying, forgive . . ."(Mark 11:25). Has someone done an unkind thing to you? If you treasure it up against them, and will not forgive them, that unforgiveness in your heart will keep your prayers from going to God. Of course you cannot just pray for anything you want. I might ask God for a million dollars but He would not give it to me because it would not be His will. "If we ask anything according to His will, He heareth us" (1 John 5:14). If we want more than anything else to do what will please The Lord Jesus, He will reveal His will and then we will be able to pray and be sure that He will answer our prayers.

NOTEBOOK SUGGESTIONS: Let the children make the initial letters as fancy as they wish. They may choose to make block letters or to illuminate the letter, or old English letters. Have them take pride in making their notebook as beautiful and artistic as possible.

RULES FOR PRAYER

1. You must be saved—John 14:6.
2. Believe He will answer your prayer—Matt. 21:22.
3. Do not hold on to any sin—Psalm 66:18.
4. Forgive others—Mark 11:25.
5. Ask according to God's will—I John 5:14.

Bank of Heaven

Pay to the order of _____

whatsoever he asks in my NAME

John 14:14

LESSON XII

ACCEPTABLE PRAYER

Point to the Lord Jesus Christ as the One Who dwells with us and with Whom we can talk constantly.

Praying and doing.
1. Our God is our Father.
2. Prayer is to be without ceasing.

WHEN the heathen pray to their idols, their thought is that they must do great things so that the idols will not hate them. They are afraid of their gods, and think they are always trying to do them harm. When they pray to them, they do not love them, for they can have no idea of a kind and loving idol.

When we pray, if we have been saved, we are not praying to an angry God, for God is our Father. He does not hate us, but loves us, and longs to do good things for us. So we love to pray to Him and to trust Him to answer our prayer in the very best way.

You remember the story of the prodigal son. He had left his father and spent all his money in bad ways. When he had nothing left, he went back to his father, to ask him to make him one of his servants, so that he would at least have enough to eat. But the father met him, and put his arms around him. He forgave him for all his bad ways, and took him back into his home again, not as a servant, but as his own son. That is the way with our Father God. We have sinned and displeased Him but He loves us and forgives us. So we come to Him in prayer, and say, "Our Father." And He is far kinder than any father on this earth, for He loves us with a perfect love.

When I was a very little child the only prayer I knew was "Now I lay me down to sleep." I used to say it every night. But afterwards I learned that praying was far more than just saying a little rhyme prayer like that. Prayer is talking with God. We can talk to Him at any time. We do not have to wait until night comes and we are going to bed to talk with Him. Before we eat, we like to stop for a moment to thank Him for giving us our food. And many other times during the day we have things to talk with Him about. There is a verse in the Bible that says: "Pray without ceasing." This does not mean that we are to be continually saying prayers, but rather that we are to be talking with God all day, just as we would talk to our dearest friend. Of course we need to have a time to talk with Him especially and ask for the things we need, and thank Him for all He has done, but many other times we can speak with Him, too.

Satan hates to have us pray. He would do anything to keep us from talking with God. So it is not surprising that we do not find it easy to pray. Every time you start to pray, Satan comes along with something else for you to do. But if we truly love God, He will send Satan away, and we shall be able to pray with joy to our Heavenly Father.

We must not pray just for ourselves, for that would be selfish. We should pray for our friends, and for those who do not know the Lord Jesus, both in this land and in the dark lands across the sea. And above all, we must not forget to tell the Lord Jesus every day that we love Him and want to please Him more than anything else in the world.

NOTEBOOK SUGGESTION: Be sure the children understand the nearness of the Lord Jesus to them.

TEST QUESTIONS ON ACCEPTABLE PRAYER ON PAGE 98.

LESSON XIII

PRACTICAL CHRISTIANITY

Point to the Lord Jesus Christ as the One Who empowers for good works.
A canoe on the ocean.
1. Good works in an unsaved person.
2. Good works in a saved person.

A CANOE is a very good boat for a lake. It is quite safe, and there is nothing more pleasant than paddling along over the smooth water on a sunny day. But a canoe would be a very bad boat for the ocean, especially in a storm. If one should be caught in a great storm on the Atlantic, in a little canoe, he would almost certainly be drowned.

Just so, people who do not know the Lord Jesus Christ do a great many "good" things. They are kind, often. They give money to the poor. They work hard. But these things are not really good at all when God looks at them. He says that they that are in the flesh—that is, those who have not been born again—*cannot* please God. They may do things that are good before men, but they cannot do things that are good before God. He says, too, that "All our righteousnesses are as filthy rags" in His sight (Isa. 64:6). If this is the way good works of unsaved people look to God, you can easily see why we cannot be saved by them. "For by grace are ye saved through faith, and that not of yourselves, it is the gift of God; *not of works*, lest any man should boast" (Eph. 2:8, 9).

What about good works, then? Does the Christian have any responsibility to do good works, or can he live just any way? The answer is to be found in another verse in Eph. 2:10—"For we are His workmanship, created in Christ Jesus, unto *good works* which God hath before ordained that we should walk in them." The very reason why He has saved us is so that we can do good works, for after the Lord has taken our sins away, works that even God can call good come into our lives.

Have you noticed that the word "works" is found twice in those two verses? Not of *works* . . . and created in Christ Jesus unto good *works.* The first kind God must curse, the second God can bless. The first works are looked upon by unsaved people as being the *root* from which they hope salvation will grow. But the Christians are saved by faith in Christ and have this salvation as the root from which the good works grow as a *fruit.* You can see that there is a vast difference between works that are a root and works that are a fruit.

This fruit is described in the Bible as a nine-fold cluster, like a bunch of grapes. "The fruit of the Spirit is love, joy, peace, longsuffering, gentleness, goodness, faith, meekness, temperance" (Gal. 5:22). Every part of this fruit should be growing in the life of each Christian.

All of us should be very practical. Someone asked Mary if her little brother was really converted. She answered, "I think he really is, for he doesn't pull the cat's tail like he used to." That is a real witness, when even the cat knows that new life has come into our hearts. That is the fruit of gentleness. If we say that we are Christians, and do not show it in the little things of life, we must ask God to keep on changing us, so that the fruit may be seen in us. A little girl who helped her mother by setting the table, always put a cracked dish at her brother's place until she was saved. Then she put it at her own place and give him the good. That is the fruit of love and goodness.

The only way to make this fruit grow in our lives is by spending time with God, studying His Word and praying, just as a garden must be watched every day if it is to produce good flowers. Have a definite time and a definite plan for reading the Bible. Read it every day, and never let a day pass. Each time you pick up the Bible ask God to use it to feed your new life and to make His fruit grow within your heart. He will answer that prayer if you really mean it.

NOTEBOOK SUGGESTIONS: Have the children give practical illustrations of the outworking of each of the nine graces that form the fruit of the Spirit.

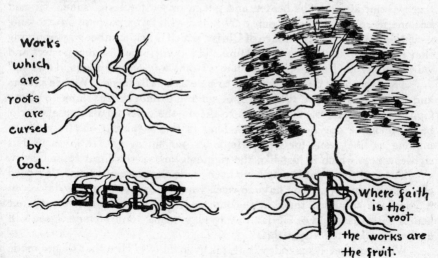

Works which are roots are cursed by God.

SELF

Where faith is the root the works are the fruit.

LESSON XIV

PRACTICAL CHRISTIANITY

Point to the Lord Jesus Christ as the One Who makes Christianity practical.

The dry pump.
1. The purpose of salvation.
    (a) To make us like Christ.
2. How can this be accomplished?

OUT in the country there is a well that used to have good, cold water in it. Today it is dry. But the old pump still stands over the well. Would you go to the pump and work the handle up and down all day long, day after day? Of course not! Only an insane person would do that. When we pump, we want to pump water, not just air.

God did not save us just in order to be doing something. There was a real reason for His saving us. If He had not had a reason, it would be like pumping at a dry well. But God's purpose is a very wonderful one. You remember the story of Peter. At the beginning he was very quick-tempered, and always getting into trouble. He was a coward, too, afraid to confess his Lord even before a servant girl. But afterwards Peter became brave, and was not afraid to be beaten and put in prison for Jesus' sake. He had become more like Jesus. Rom. 8:29 tells us that His purpose in choosing us is to conform us to the image of Christ, which is just another way of saying that He is going to make us like Him. The Lord Jesus Christ is perfect and we are surely far from perfect. What is God's way of making us like Jesus?

The first thing He does for us is to save us by His blood. We are sinners and have an old nature that is full of sin and cannot do anything to please God. So God sent the Lord Jesus to die on the cross for us and shed His blood to make our hearts clean. That is the beginning of His work of making us like Jesus for when He takes our sin away, He gives us His righteousness which is just like the righteousness of the Lord Jesus Christ.

But even after our hearts have been made clean, we often sin. We need cleansing every day. You have to wash your hands many times a day, even if you have scrubbed them in the morning. God keeps on cleansing our hearts with the blood of Christ, day by day. In 1 John 1:7 and 9 you will find verses that tell about this.

We cannot see Jesus today, but it is by looking at Him that we are made like Him. But that is impossible, you say. How can we look at Him if we cannot see Him? Take your Bible and look at 2 Cor. 3:18. There we read that as we behold in a glass (a mirror) the glory of the Lord, we are changed into the same image. Sometimes you look into a mirror that is placed just right and can see things around a corner, or behind you. So we see Jesus by looking in a mirror and that mirror is the Bible. Every time we read the Bible it is looking at Jesus for He is the One about Whom the whole book is written. You try it and see. Read His Word, and God will make you more like Him.

Then, too, we have the Holy Spirit in us to do this work. 2 Cor. 3:18 says that it is done "as by the Spirit of the Lord." Talking with the Lord Jesus will make you more like Him, too. He loves you and wants you to pray to Him. Prayer will change you and make you more like Him.

NOTEBOOK SUGGESTIONS: Let the children give their own answers to the questions. Help them if necessary. Encourage them to write the verse artistically. A neat notebook can be made to the glory of the Lord.

    I. Why did God save us?
       (a) God saved us to make us like the Lord Jesus Christ—Rom. 8:29.
    II. How does God make us like Christ?
       (a) By saving us.
       (b) By cleansing us day by day.
       (c) By His Word.
       (d) By His Spirit.

Beholding as in a glass the glory of the Lord, we are changed...

II Corinthians 3:18

LESSON XV

PRACTICAL CHRISTIANITY

Point to the Lord Jesus Christ as the One Who makes us witnesses.

Getting ready for Heaven.
1. Why God leaves us in the world.
2. How we can be witnesses.

THE moment we are saved we are ready for Heaven. Having our hearts washed clean by the blood of Christ, makes us ready for Heaven, and that happens, you know, the moment you believe in Him as your own Saviour. We are just as ready for Heaven after we have been saved one minute as after we have been saved fifty years. Our readiness consists in what Christ is and did for us and not in what we are or do for ourselves.

Why do you suppose, then, that He does not take us to Heaven right away? Why does He leave us here in this world? Surely Heaven is much better than this world, and it would be a great deal better to go there the minute we are saved. But God has a good reason for keeping us here, and the Lord Jesus tells about it in Acts 1:8. He says, "And ye shall be witnesses unto me." That is what He wants each one of us who belong to Him, to be.

What is a witness? A witness is someone who tells what he has seen or heard or knows. As witnesses to the Lord Jesus Christ we tell what we know through His Word about Him. What do we know that we can tell others?

First we know that all men are sinners. Rom. 3:23 makes that very plain indeed. Then we know that God loves us, though we are sinners. Rom. 5:8 tells us that. Then we know that God's love was so great that He gave His only begotten Son to die for us. John 3:16 is the verse for that. And we know that if men will believe that He died for them, He will save them, and give them eternal life. Acts 16:31 is the verse for this great fact.

If we really know these things, it is our business to tell those who do not know. Some of them will believe, and some will not believe. That is always the way. It is not our work to make people believe, but it is our work to tell them about the Lord. It is only God Himself that can give them faith, for we read in Eph. 2:8, "For by grace are ye saved through faith, and that (faith) not of yourselves, it is the gift of God." We cannot give them faith, but the Holy Spirit will, if we are faithful in our witnessing.

Some people are very successful witnesses. By that we mean that many of those to whom they speak accept the Lord Jesus Christ as their Saviour.

How is it that some are better than others in this work? It is not because some are wiser or more educated than others. It is because some have given themselves more completely to the Holy Spirit. It is His power that makes us good witnesses. Acts 1:8 says, "And ye shall receive power, after that the Holy Ghost is come upon you, and ye shall be witnesses unto Me." We cannot be witnesses without the power of the Holy Spirit.

When Jesus called some of His disciples to follow Him, they were in a boat fishing. He said to them, "Follow Me, and I will make you fishers of men" (Matt. 4:19). They did follow Him, and they were very successful witnesses. That is what being a "fisher of men" means. At Pentecost, when Peter, one of the fishermen, preached to the people, three thousand were saved. That was because of the power of the Holy Spirit. Peter, by himself, could never have done it. The same Holy Spirit is ready to help us, if we will let Him.

NOTEBOOK SUGGESTIONS: Let the children draw their illustration. Try to get a variety of ideas. This one is given just to help out in case some one needs an idea.

Tell others!

Good News!

Matthew 4:19

Follow me and I will make you fishers of men.

Go!

LESSON XVI

PRACTICAL CHRISTIANITY

Point to the Lord Jesus Christ as the One Who should be Lord of our lives.

How to be saved.
1. Christ as Saviour.
2. Christ as Lord.
3. Why we should yield to Him.
4. What He will do with our lives.

THE only way we can be saved is through the Lord Jesus Christ. He died on the cross to take our punishment for us. If we believe that, then He is our Saviour, and we are safe for ever, for He has promised to keep us. But being saved is not all there is to the Christian life, any more than getting into a boat is the whole of a journey across the ocean. You cannot cross the ocean without getting on the boat, but if no one did anything after they got on the boat, it would be a queer kind of voyage. Some Christians are living that sort of life—just drifting around, without much of any purpose. That is not what God meant us to do. He has a plan for us.

When men build a great building, they do not put the wood and bricks and cement together just any old way. They have a plan. Perhaps you have seen a builder's plans. They are usually what are called "blue prints," great pieces of blue paper with white lines on them, showing just exactly how the building is to be made. God has a plan for your life that is just as exact as any blue print that was ever made. In Eph. 2:10, we read, "And we are His workmanship, created in Christ Jesus unto good works which God hath before ordained that we should walk in them." Just think— God made a plan for your life long before you were born. It is a wonderful plan, the very best that could be made.

Since God has a plan for you, what should you do? Some Christians make the mistake of thinking that they must run their own lives. What would happen, if someone who knew nothing about building, should come and try to build a great skyscraper? They would ruin the plans, and the building would be a failure. It takes someone who *knows how* to do a thing like that. And it takes Someone Who knows how to build our lives according to His plan. That Someone is God. We cannot build our lives the right way. Only God can do that.

What should we do then? The answer is in one great word. *Yield.*

That means to give our lives, as well as our hearts to God, and ask Him to manage them. That means we will not have our own way, but His way.

Why should we give our lives to Him? There are many reasons. If Jesus died for us, we are not our own. We are bought with the price of His blood. He has justified us and made us His children. We have no right to keep on with our own way, when He has His way for us. His way will be a wonderful way, far better than any way we could plan. Sometimes we may think we could plan better, but that is a great mistake. He knows all things, and He will lead us in the right way.

First of all, we must give our whole lives to Him, saying, "Lord Jesus, Thou hast died for me, and I give Thee, not only my heart, but my life, to be all for Thee." And then, day after day, hour after hour, minute after minute, we must keep that promise. Satan will tempt us to do wrong, but we must tell him no, for we belong to another. He, our Lord Jesus, is able to keep us and He will do it.

NOTEBOOK SUGGESTION:

How can we know God's plans for our lives?
God has a plan for each of us—Eph. 2:10.
We can know this plan only if we let Him be our Lord, obeying Him as a soldier must obey His captain. First we must decide that He is to manage our lives, and then each day we must let Him do it, so we will not get out of His way.

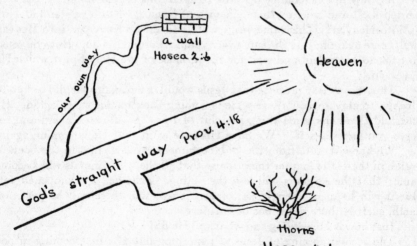

TEST QUESTIONS ON PRACTICAL CHRISTIANITY ON PAGE 99.

LESSON XVII

SECOND COMING OF CHRIST

Point to the Lord Jesus Christ as the coming One.

The teacher should read W. E. Blackstones "Jesus is Coming."
Christ leaves the earth.
1. The promise.
2. The order of events.

AFTER the resurrection of the Lord Jesus Christ, His disciples saw Him many times. He talked with them of many things, but He did not remain with them for ever. The day came when He was ready to leave them. He took them with Him outside the city to a mountain called the Mount of Olives. There, He promised that they should receive power when the Holy Spirit came upon them and that they should be His witnesses. As He spoke to them He rose from the earth, and He ascended up to Heaven. The disciples stood watching Him, till a cloud hid Him from their sight. Then they still stood looking up where they had seen Him disappear. Perhaps they expected that He would come back again.

As they stood looking up into Heaven two angels stood by them in white robes, and said to them, Ye men of Galilee, why do ye stand looking up into Heaven? This same Jesus who is taken up from you into Heaven shall come again in just the same way you have seen Him go. But you must go back to Jerusalem and wait for the promise of the Holy Spirit which He gave you.

This was a clear promise that Jesus would come again. He did not go to Heaven to stay there forever. He is coming back to this earth again. He had told them the same thing in John 14:1-3—"I will come again and receive you unto myself." We have His sure word that He is coming again.

We know it, too, from the Old Testament. Let us find in the book of Isaiah in the 11th Chapter the promise that all the wild animals will become tame; that the serpents will lose their sting. That has not happened yet. But it will happen when Jesus comes. Then, too, there will be peace on earth, such as there never has been before.

Just how is He coming and what will He do?

The second coming of Jesus is something like His first coming in one way. It does not take place all at once. At His first coming, there was the star and the angels' song, and the temptation and the miracles and the transfiguration and the crucifixion and the resurrection. When He comes again, many things will happen, too.

Now we are living centuries after the birth of Jesus and we do not know how long it will be before He comes back. But some day, and it might be today, Jesus will come back; not all the way to the earth, but in the air. He will call us Himself and all the believers who have died will be raised from the dead. All believers who are alive will be changed and made like Jesus. So He will take us to Heaven with Him. We read all about that in 1 Thess. 4:13-18. Let us turn to it and read it together.

After that great event come seven years when the earth will be having a terrible time. Can you imagine what this world would be like without a single Christian in it? For that is what will happen, you know, when Jesus comes. He will take every believer out of the world. Great judgments will be poured out on the earth, there will be famine and earthquake, disease and war. At the end of the seven years there will be a great war—the greatest of all. In the midst of that war Jesus will come back to earth, from Heaven, bringing us with Him. He will stop the war and judge the nations, and set up on the earth, His own kingdom which will last for a thousand years.

NOTEBOOK SUGGESTIONS: Perhaps the group could all sing "When He Cometh." Draw the music first.

LESSON XVIII

SECOND COMING OF CHRIST

Point to the Lord Jesus as the One for Whom we wait daily.

OUR lesson today is about the part of the second coming of the Lord Jesus which is called the *rapture*. It is the first thing that will happen among the events of His coming.

First of all, what is it? There are several places in the Scripture where we read about it, and where we can find out clearly just what it is. You remember the great passage in the 14th chapter of John. The Lord Jesus had told His disciples that He was going away, and they were very sad. But He wanted to comfort them. He told them not to let their hearts be troubled, for He was going to prepare a place for them. And if He prepared a place for them, He said, He would come again and receive them unto Himself, so that they might be with Him forever. After He had gone away from them into Heaven, the Holy Spirit explained more about this coming.

When Paul had been in Thessalonica he had taught the believers that they could look for the Lord to return at any moment. When they got up in the morning they could say to themselves and to the Lord, Perhaps He will be back today! Maybe He will be here before evening! And at night as they went to sleep they could say, Perhaps He will be here before morning! Then there came a day when some of their loved ones, a mother or father, a brother or sister, died. They immediately asked Paul if these loved ones, whose bodies had been put in their graves, would be left behind, and if the living ones should see the Lord first. Paul answers them (1 Thess. 4:13-18), that they are not to be ignorant about these loved ones, because God does not want believers to sorrow like unbelievers who have no hope of resurrection. Just as surely as we believe that Jesus died and rose again, so surely may we believe that he will bring with Him at His second coming, the spirits of the loved ones who have died. We shall not go first, but in a moment, in the twinkling of an eye (and that is even quicker than a wink!), the dead *in Christ* shall rise *first*. Note that the dead out of Christ do not rise then. As soon as the bodies of these Christian dead are out of their graves and their spirits, brought from Heaven, are in them, all the living believers will be changed, to become like the Lord Jesus.

Of course only believers will be caught up to meet Him. You have seen a magnet work, haven't you? It will pick up steel or iron, but it will not pick up tin or nickel. If you had a little heap of iron filings, mixed with sawdust, the magnet would draw all the iron filings to meet it, but the sawdust would lie on the table just as though no magnet had come near it. So, when the Lord Jesus comes, those who have been born again will go to meet Him. The unsaved will not.

In 1 Cor. 15:51-53 we learn a little more about what is to happen to believers. Paul writes, Behold, I tell you a secret. We shall not all die, but we shall all be changed. In a moment, in the twinkling of an eye, at the sound of the last trumpet, the dead will be raised incorruptible, and we shall be changed. What will this change be? How will we be changed? In 1 John 3:2 it says we shall be made like the Lord Jesus when we see Him as He is. And Phil. 3:21 says that when the Lord Jesus comes, He will change our bodies so that they may be made like His glorious body. All our sins will be gone. We shall not even have our old nature any longer.

It will be a wonderful thing to see Jesus and to be made like Him. We are waiting every day for Him to come, for He says, "Behold, I come quickly." He did not tell us when He would come back, but left us to wait for Him every day. Today may be the day He will come. Let's not do anything that we would not want to be doing when He comes.

NOTEBOOK SUGGESTIONS: Let the children draw as you explain and review each point as they draw. There should be short rulers available for the children to draw the lines, or if they prefer, let them draw freehand, as in the sketch below.

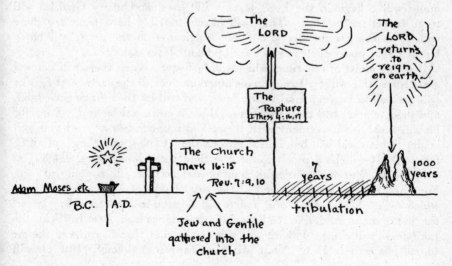

LESSON XIX

SECOND COMING OF CHRIST

Point to the Lord Jesus as our Coming King

When Jesus comes.
1. The Great Tribulation.
2. Christ's return to the earth.

IT WILL be wonderful for believers when Jesus comes, for then they will go to be with Him for ever. Their bodies will be made like His, and they shall live for ever with Him. Nothing could be better than that. But can you think what it will be for those who are not believers? For they will be left behind. Not one of those who do not believe in the Lord Jesus Christ will be taken when He comes. Some day all Christians will disappear. The unbelievers will be looking for them, but they will not find them. They will be gone.

What an awful place the world would be if there were no Christians in it! All the wicked people will be able to do what they like. And then, too, God is going to begin to judge the earth. Judgment after judgment will come. There will be war, famine, sickness, death. In the midst of it all many will believe in the Lord Jesus. All Jews, and many Gentiles will come to believe in Him. They will have a terribly hard time, for there will be so many unbelievers, and the judgments on the earth will be so terrible, that many of them will have to die for Jesus' sake.

In the midst of this time, which will last seven years, there will come a great ruler. He will try to set up his kingdom over all the earth. At first he will pretend to be very kind to the Jews, and will let them have their land, and their temple, and their sacrifices. But they will not be happy long, for he will break his agreement with them, and immediately a great war will begin. The world will be divided into two great sides, and they will all be fighting. It will be a much worse war than these world wars which you study now. But the wonderful thing is that neither side is going to win. For when the war is at its worst at the great battle of Armageddon, about which we read in God's Word, a sign will be seen in Heaven—the sign of the Son of man. And, like the lightning, that shines from East to West, the Lord Jesus will come. This time it will not be that He will come in the air to call His own to Him. That will have happened already. But He will

come all the way to the earth.   When He left the disciples, long before, He
ascended from the Mount of Olives. He is coming back to the same mountain. His feet shall stand on the Mount of Olives. And we are coming back
with Him, for we have His promise that we shall never have to leave Him
again forever.

When He comes, the battle stops, and He judges the nations. Those
who have rejected the Gospel, which the Jews, His brethren, have preached,
will be judged. And those who have accepted that Gospel will be rewarded.
And then He will set up His Kingdom on the earth. You cannot imagine
anything so wonderful as that Kingdom will be. All the earth will be
changed. There will be no more deserts. They will all be like flower gardens.
There will be no more wild animals. They will be tame, every one of them.
Then, if you like, you can have a lion or a tiger for a pet. Babies will be
able to put their hands down the holes made by serpents that used to be
poisonous, without fear of harm, for there will be no more poison. And
best of all, the Lord will rule, and make every one obey Him. There will
be no more war and no more fighting. All will be Peace because the Prince
of Peace, our Lord Jesus will be here, and will be the King.

NOTEBOOK SUGGESTION: (Same as in Lesson XVIII.)

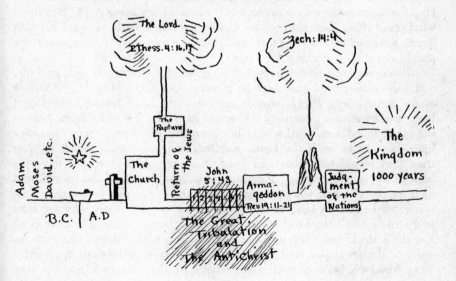

LESSON XX

SECOND COMING OF CHRIST

Point to the Lord Jesus Christ as the One Whose coming makes us zealous of good works.

Practical effect of His coming.
1. To live daily for Him.
2. To have joy no matter what happens.
3. To witness to others.

WE KNOW that the Lord Jesus may come at any moment, to take us to be with Himself. Does this make any difference in the way we live? We are not afraid of His coming, for we know that He can see us just as truly today, while He is in Heaven, as He will when He comes and we can see Him. But the moment of His coming is going to be the most wonderful moment that there has ever been. But if, when He comes, we are doing something that would not please Him, or saying something unkind or untrue, or if we are in some place that He would not like, it will spoil that beautiful moment for us. It is not that He would not take us to be with Him if we were doing something that would displease Him, for He takes us because we are saved, not because we are being good. But think what a sad thing it would be if we had to meet Him with our head hanging down, ashamed to see His face! And since He may come any moment, we should always be waiting for Him.

Some very sad things happen in this world. People get sick, and die, and leave their loved ones here to mourn. But Christians do not sorrow as the world does. People who do not know the Lord Jesus Christ do not have any hope at all, for they will never have the joy of living in heaven with their loved ones. But when Christians die, their friends know that they have gone to be with the Lord, and that they are much, much happier than they would be if they still lived on earth. And then they have the hope of the Lord's coming. For since we believe that the Lord Jesus Christ died for us, and rose again, we know that those who die, trusting in Him, will come back with Him when He comes for us. For those who are alive and remain until the Lord comes will not go before those who have died. For the Lord Himself will descend from Heaven with a shout, and with the voice of the archangel, and the trumpet of God; and the dead in Christ— those who have believed in Him and have died, shall be raised from the dead first. Then we who are still alive and who remain until the Lord's coming, shall be caught up into the air together with those who were dead, to meet the Lord in the clouds. And so we shall all be with the Lord forever. It is these words that God has given us when there is sorrow.

But in all our joy in the Lord's coming, we cannot forget those who are not saved, and who will be left behind when He comes. That will be a terrible time for unbelievers. And we want, so much, to let them know about the Lord Jesus Christ, so that they will believe and be saved, and go to meet Him when He comes. We know that not all the world will be converted, so we are not just trying to make things better here, but we are trying to rescue all we can from Satan before the Lord comes. If we really mean this, we will be telling our friends about Him, bringing them with us so that they can hear about our Saviour. And we will pray for them, and for missionaries who are preaching to so many about Him, asking God to bless them, and to bring many, many, many to Himself.

NOTEBOOK SUGGESTION: As the children draw the following illustration, explain that the spirits of the righteous dead are with God in Paradise and are given a new body to live in when Christ raises their old bodies. The bodies of those who had not died will be changed so that all will have an undying and incorruptible body like the one of the Lord Jesus when he was raised from the dead.

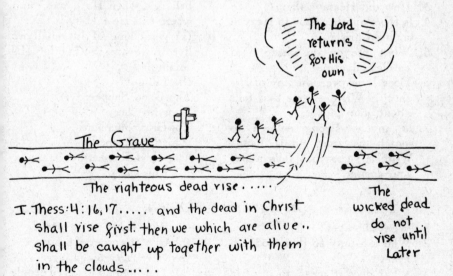

The Lord returns for His own

The Grave

The righteous dead rise.....

I. Thess: 4:16,17 ..... and the dead in Christ shall rise first. then we which are alive.. shall be caught up together with them in the clouds.....

The wicked dead do not rise until Later

TEST QUESTIONS ON SECOND COMING OF CHRIST ON PAGE 99.

TEST QUESTIONS—COURSE TWO

CHRIST OUR DELIVERER

1. Of what were we servants before we believed in the Lord Jesus?
2. Who are the slaves of sin?
3. (a) Who can free us from this terrible master?
   (b) How did He do it?
4. Do Christians ever sin?
5. (a) Is it a sin to be tempted?
   (b) How do you know?
6. Can we get rid of the old nature in this life?
7. When will we lose the old nature?
8. What are the two best things you know about Heaven?
9. How can Christians keep from sinning?
10. Why cannot the old sinful nature go to Heaven?

SHEPHERD WORK OF CHRIST

1. Who are the sheep of the Lord Jesus?
2. Why did they need to be saved?
3. How did He save them?
4. Is there another door to Heaven besides Christ?
5. What else do the sheep need besides salvation?
6. Does Jesus ever lose any of His sheep? Write a verse that tells about your answer.
7. Is anyone strong enough to snatch us from Jesus hand? Write a verse that tells about your answer.
8. Will we ever see the Chief Shepherd? If so—when?
9. What is He going to give to believers when He comes—and where will He take us?
10. (a) What kind of life shall we live if we are waiting for His coming?
    (b) Fill out—
    The Good Shepherd.......... for his sheep.
    The Great Shepherd.......... for his sheep.
    The Chief Shepherd.......... for his sheep.

ACCEPTABLE PRAYER

1. What is prayer?
2. Who can pray so that God will hear?
3. What does it mean to pray in Jesus' name?
4. (a) Who helps us to pray?
   (b) Give the order of prayer.
5. Give five rules for prayer.
6. (a) To whom do unsaved people really pray?

(b) What people are unsaved?

7. Tell at least five things you can give thanks for, and five things you can ask for when you pray.

8. (a) Give one Bible verse about prayer.

(b) What does it mean?

9. What or who keeps us from praying as we ought?

10. In praying what is the most important thing that we should tell our Lord Jesus every day?

PRACTICAL CHRISTIANITY

1. What difference is there between good works in an unsaved man and good works in a Christian?

2. For what purpose did God save us?

3. Why does God leave Christians in this world?

4. Tell four ways by which God makes us like Christ.

5. What is a witness?

6. As a witness for Christ, what can you tell people?

7. By whom should a Christian's life be managed?

8. Name at least four parts of the fruit of the Spirit.

9. Tell one way in which you know Christ is working in your everyday life.

10. How would you tell an unconverted friend how to become a Christian?

THE SECOND COMING OF CHRIST

1. Draw a diagram to show the parts of the Lord's second coming.

2. Can you tell of at least two places in the Bible where the Second Coming is mentioned?

3. What is the rapture?

4. What will happen to living believers when the Lord comes?

5. What will happen to the dead in Christ when Christ comes?

6. What will happen to the unsaved dead when Christ comes?

7. What will take place on the earth after the rapture?

9. What will end the Great Tribulation?

8. Tell something about the Millennial kingdom, how long it will last, and what kind of time it will be.

10. Name three results that come in the lives of those who are waiting for the Lord's coming.

COURSE THREE

LESSON I

THE BIBLE
God's Revelation

GOD knows everything, and God can do anything. If He had not wanted us to know something He could have kept it from us; all that He wants us to know He tells us. Men did not know anything about God except that which He chose to tell them. He has told us about Himself in two ways, in the world round about us and in the Bible.

The world round about us cannot tell us very much about God. It tells us that God is great and wise; and it tells us that, over and over again, in many different ways. We can look at the power of the waves on the beach, or the power of the wind in the trees, or the power of a growing plant to split a rock in two, or the power of a river to wash away its bank, or the power of the sun to lift water up to the clouds, but all of these examples are the one lesson of the power of God, told over and over again. We can look through a magnifying glass and see that God never made two leaves alike, nor two grains of sand alike, nor two snowflakes alike; we can look with a telescope and see that no two stars are alike; we can see with our eyes that no two people are exactly alike, no two clouds are alike. All of this tells us that God is very wise, and knows everything.

All people can see the power and the wisdom of God in nature. Even the heathen in the heart of Africa can know that, if they only stop to think about it. God says in the Bible, "That which may be known of God is manifest in them; for God hath shewed it unto them. For the invisible things of Him from the creation of the world are clearly seen, being understood by the things that are made, even His eternal power and Godhead; so that they are without excuse" (Rom. 1:19, 20). This tells us that all men should have said to themselves: How wonderful is the God that made the sky, the rain, the hills, the trees, the world and all that is in it, and Who made me! I will have to love such a God and always obey Him, for One that is so powerful and wise must be very good, and I am not good, so I will try to be what He would want me to be. But no man has ever done that, so God says that all men are without excuse.

The Bible has the answers to all of the questions that can ever come into the mind of any man about creation, life, death, the thoughts and the mind of man, the past, the present and the future. Man could never know these things by himself, but God has told him these things in this Book which is a revelation. The word revelation means an unveiling. If you saw a lady with a heavy veil you might not know whether her eyes were brown or gray. What would you think of two boys who would argue and argue about the shade of the eyes of a lady whom they had never seen! One might say that he believed her eyes were brown because she was very tall and he had once known a very tall woman who had brown eyes. The other might say that her eyes were gray because she had on a blue dress and he had once known a woman with a blue dress whose eyes were gray. That all may sound very reasonable to some people, but if the lady takes her veil off and you see that her eyes are very blue eyes, all of the arguments of the small boys would become silly.

So God has taken off the veil from many questions. In the Bible we find how the world came into being, how sin entered the universe, how man was created, how man became a sinner, how God loves man, how Christ came to die for us, how we may be saved, how the Lord Jesus is coming again, how God is going to bring joy to this world at last and how we are going to be in Heaven with Him for ever. There are many other things that are to be found in this wonderful book, but it is enough to say that all that God thinks it necessary for man to know about himself and about God is in this Bible.

NOTEBOOK SUGGESTIONS: Be sure the children realize that a supernatural Book can be understood only by born again people. The unsaved people will always keep their question-marks about the past, the future and God. Have the children write beneath the picture 1 Cor. 2:10(a) "But God hath revealed them unto us by His Spirit."

LESSON II

THE BIBLE

Inspiration

WHEN God took the veil from things that man could not know by himself, He began to tell man about it. Adam knew some things about God, about salvation, about eternal life, long before there was a Bible. Abel knew about the blood sacrifice and Enoch knew about the second coming of Christ (Jude 14). Yet none of these things had been written down in the Bible as yet.

About the time of Moses, God began to choose men to write down all that He wanted them to know about themselves and about Himself. They had to write about things of which they never could have known the answers by themselves.

If we asked you to write a composition about what you did on the fifth of August, 1939, you might make a mistake in remembering and confuse it with something you did on the 30th of July! And if God had asked Moses to write down something that he had done forty years before, Moses might have made a mistake. But God breathed upon Moses with a special power that is called Inspiration, and kept Moses from making any mistakes when he wrote about things he had done himself, years before.

Then, of course, you could never write about something that you knew nothing about. If we told you that there was a boy named John Smith who lived in Australia in 1870, and that he had never been heard of from the time he got off the boat from England when he was eight years old, and asked you to write a *true* story of his life from then on, you would not be able to do it. But if you could have God whisper in your ear and give you the very words to write, you would not have any difficulty in writing correctly. So when God told Moses to write about the creation, and about the coming of sin into the world, God had to reveal the truth to Moses and then inspire him to write it down without error.

Again, if we asked you to write a story about a trip to Mars in the year 2500, you could not do it, except as a tale of imagination. There will be new words in use then that we do not know. What would your great-great-grandfather say if he came into your house as you have it today? He might watch you at the radio and say, "He took a button on the end of a string and put it into a hole in the wall and then turned a knob and music came out of a box." That is a pretty good description of the radio, though it does not use the technical words which every boy knows today. We would say that we plugged into a socket, then dialed for the broadcasting station we wanted until we got the right wave-length, and listened to a radio program.   So, in the Bible, God took some of the prophets forward, through visions, and told them of things that are still in the future, and made them describe it in the simple language of their time.   We already understand some of these things in the language of our day, and we will understand still more as time goes on.   For example, the prophet Ezekiel tells us about some angel beings in language that is hard for us to understand now, and John describes Heaven in a way that will be simple to us when we see it.

All of these men who wrote the Bible did so because God chose them for it and inspired them so that they would make no mistakes at all whether they wrote of facts they knew about, or of things in the past and the future that He had to reveal to them especially.   The Holy Spirit tells us through Peter that "the prophecy came not in old time by the will of man; but holy men of God spake as they were moved by the Holy Spirit" (2 Pet. 1:21).   The word for "moved" really means carried along, like a boat is carried by a wind.   That is the way the breath of God carried the men who wrote the Bible.   Sometimes they did not know the meaning of what they had written.   Daniel wrote his prophecy and then asked the Lord what it meant (Dan. 12:8), and all of the men who wrote the Bible studied it to find out what it meant.   Even angels would like to know all that is in the Bible (1 Pet. 1:10-12).

NOTEBOOK SUGGESTION: Draw the Bible and the light of the Spirit first, then the other objects will space properly.

LESSON III

THE BIBLE

The Word Convicting and Converting

THE Bible is a supernatural Book. No other book was ever given by God. No other book contains any of God's unveiling and God never breathed upon any other men than those who wrote the Bible, to keep them from error in their work.

The Bible is the story of *Man's Complete Ruin in Sin* and *God's Perfect Remedy in Christ.* You might call that, all of the Bible in ten words. Memorize those ten words, for there is nothing in the Bible that does not have to do with one of those two phrases.

The reason that some men hate the Bible is because it shows them what their heart really is, and wounds their pride beyond cure. There is a story about a girl who was very ugly, so ugly that she never wanted to look at herself in a mirror. She hated the sight of a mirror, and would not have one in her room. We know, of course, that her hatred of mirrors did not make her any more beautiful. Another little girl thought herself to be so pretty that she looked in a mirror every chance she had and turned her head one way and another in order to see herself better. It was only when she read her Bible that she found that God was not pleased with her heart any more than He was pleased with the heart of an ugly girl.

A little boy in the South of France went into the kitchen one day as his mother was putting away some glasses of jam that had just been made. She had to go out on an errand and told the little boy that he must not go near the jam. While she was gone he got a chair and went to the cupboard, dipped his finger in each of the glasses and licked it each time. Suddenly he heard his mother coming back. He closed the cupboard, put the chair in its place, and went into the next room. His mother called him to her and asked him why he had disobeyed her. He lied to her and told her that he had not touched the jam. She looked at him steadily. He had been looking her straight in the eye. He then began looking at her mouth, then at the buttons on her dress, then at her belt buckle, then at her shoes. Then he looked down at his own shoes, and, as his head got lower and lower, he suddenly saw the reason why his mother had been so sure of what he had been doing while she was out. On his coat was a big spot of jam! This is just what the Bible does for man. It shows him the spot that is within his breast; it reveals to him that he has a sinful heart.

He would never have known it unless God had given the Bible. Paul says that he would never have known what sin was except for the fact that God gave the law. He would not have known that it was wrong to desire wrong things if God had not said, Thou shalt not covet (Rom. 7:7).

It is the Bible that tells us that our good deeds cannot please God because He is holy and we are sinners. It is the Bible that tells us that our character cannot save us. It is the Bible that tells us that we are not saved by works lest any man should boast (Eph. 2:9). These are not things that men would think out for themselves, and most unbelievers hope that they can be saved by what they do, though God says they cannot.

When God, the Holy Spirit, saves someone, He does it always the same way. He takes some verse in the Bible about God's holiness or some verse in the Bible about how terrible sin really is. Then he uses this to stir up the unbeliever's heart so that he is convicted of his sin, of God's righteousness and of the judgment of God against sin (John 16:8). Then when the unbeliever knows what God thinks about his sin, God reveals to him, and always through the Bible, that He, God, is perfectly satisfied with the death of Jesus Christ instead of the death of the sinner.

What the brush is to the artist in painting a picture, what the hammer is to the carpenter in driving a nail, what water is to the laundress in washing clothes, so the Bible is to God in saving a soul.

NOTEBOOK SUGGESTIONS: Make a heart so that the children can trace its outline. Let them choose a verse about sin and one about salvation to write beneath their picture.

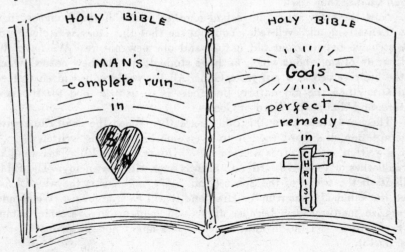

LESSON IV

THE BIBLE

The Word Building and Strengthening

THE study of God's Word is the only way whereby a Christian can have his life grow like the life of the Lord Jesus.

The Bible says the young Christian is a babe, and that the babe is to grow by the sincere milk of the Word (1 Pet. 2:2). When I was visiting some missionary friends in India, I saw a fight between a cobra and a mongoose. A cobra is a poisonous snake and a mongoose is a small animal, as large as a good-sized kitten. The cobra was coiled with his head in the air and the mongoose came nearer and nearer until, suddenly, the cobra struck at the mongoose who leaped back just in time. I thought, at first, that the snake had been able to bite the animal. Each time the snake struck and missed it lifted its head once more, on guard. The mongoose went forwards and backwards so many times that the snake began to get tired, and its thrusts were much slower than before. Finally as the cobra struck slowly the mongoose leaped into the air and sunk its teeth into the back of the serpent's neck (if we can talk about a snake having a neck!) and held on for dear life. The snake writhed and coiled itself about the mongoose, but it was too late. In a little while the great snake, which could have swallowed the mongoose whole, lay dead, killed by a little animal much smaller than itself.

Now the story might have had another ending if the mongoose had not been strong and well-fed. You can see that this story is a picture of the struggle between our old nature and our new nature. We have the old nature of sin, about which we have studied, and the new nature which is the life received as a gift from God. All the world is organized to feed and strengthen the old nature, but there is *only one* food for the new nature, and that is the Word of God.

The Lord Jesus knew the Bible perfectly. When the devil came with a temptation, the Lord used it to overcome him. "It is written . . ." "It is written . . ." "It is written . . ." (Matt. 4:4, 7, 10). This was like three flashes of a sharp sword, and all was over with the enemy. The Bible calls itself the sword of the Spirit (Eph. 6:17), and this is the way Christ used the Bible. It was true for Him, and it will be true for us. We should memorize many verses, because these will help us to overcome Satan. "Thy Word have I hid in mine heart, that I might not sin against Thee" (Ps. 66:18).

Then the Bible is a lamp for our feet and a light for our path (Ps. 119: 105). You might have to cross a moor at night, or go along a dangerous path. You would not need a great searchlight, strong enough to pick out an airplane in the sky. A little lamp, strong enough to show you your path would be enough to take you, step by step, all the way home. So God's Word is a lamp that shines around our feet and on our path. If we will study it, we shall always know our next step, and then the next one, and we shall surely stay in the will of God.

When we remember that we are witnesses, the Word of God is our only tool for that work. God said to Jeremiah, "Is not My Word like as a fire? and like a hammer that breaketh the rock in pieces?" (Jer. 23:29). If you speak to others in your own words, they may say, "Who are you to speak to me about what I do?" But if you quote the Bible you will find that it can do what your words can never do and that it will enable you to be a true witness for the Lord.

NOTEBOOK SUGGESTIONS: Let each child choose one verse of the 119th Psalm to write out under the pictures.

MILK

Thy Word is a lamp.....
Psalm 119:105

... like a hammer

....like as a fire.
Jer. 23:29

.... milk of the Word
I Peter 2:2

Ephesians 6:17   sword.... which is the Word.

TEST QUESTIONS ON THE BIBLE ON PAGE 142

LESSON V

FREEDOM

Point to the Lord Jesus Christ as the only One Who can loosen the chains of bondage.

MEN do not like to be in bondage. At the time of the Civil War America took her stand against slavery. We do not believe in the principle of one man's being owned by another. You have never seen a slave, for they were freed before you were born.

Yet in another sense we have seen slaves, for God says that all unbelievers are slaves. Before you and I were saved we, too, were servants of sin. The Lord Jesus said, "Whosoever committeth sin is the servant of sin." Since all have sinned, all are servants of sin. Slavery is a terrible thing, but it is nothing compared to the slavery of sin. Have you ever seen men with faces that hardly look like human faces, so scarred are they by the results of sin. Men and women with minds ruined are in insane asylums. The hospital wards contain many who are there simply because they have destroyed their bodies by sin. Sin is a terrible master (Rom. 6:17).

It was sin that transformed Lucifer, the powerful and beautiful angel, into Satan, our greatest enemy. It was sin that sent Adam and Eve out of the lovely garden of Eden to suffer and finally to die. It was sin that nailed our Lord Jesus Christ to the cross, and made Him suffer and die there for us. Sin is the most terrible thing in the universe. And everyone who has ever sinned is the slave of sin. That means that you and I are sin's slaves, too, unless we have been made free.

Sin is like the chain which binds a slave. And to what does the chain of sin bind us? It is a terrible thing, but the other end of that chain is attached to the enemy of God and the enemy of our souls—Satan. 2 Tim. 2:26 says that we are "taken captive by him at his will." Just as you can lead around a dog by a chain, so Satan leads around by the chain of sin those who are his captives. And he is a strong master, as well as a very cruel one. He is much stronger than you or I, and we cannot escape from him by our own strength. He hates us, and hates God, and wants to make us miserable and unhappy. Sometimes he may seem to give us a good time for a little while, but he always jerks us back into unhappiness and misery by that strong chain of sin. An old colored mammy used to say, "I done serve de debil for forty years, and he nebber pay me off once." The Devil is a hard master.

When you have a dog on a chain, you know you must have a collar on his neck.   Satan has a collar on us to which he attaches the chain of sin, and by which he holds us.   That collar is "self."   Eph. 2:3 says that we, before we believed in the Lord Jesus Christ, lived among the children of wrath, and were fulfilling the desires of the *flesh*—which means, of the old sinful self.   It was a tight uncomfortable collar, but we did not like to give it up.   Satan had put it on so tightly that we could not get rid of it.

There is only one way to get out of this slavery—through the great Liberator, the Lord Jesus Christ.   When Christ wished to free us, He had to give His life for us.   Our freedom was purchased at a great cost, and given us as a gift.   Now we have a new master, the Lord Jesus Christ.

When He died on the cross, He took away the power of the old slave holder, Satan.   He removed the chain of sin, and broke off the old collar of self, so that now we can be free—free from Satan, sin, and self.

NOTEBOOK SUGGESTION: Let the children choose which of the verses indicated in the teacher's outline they wish to write in their notebook.   Giving them a choice makes them consider the meaning of the verses.

Three-fold   Slavery
— to —

Sin   Self   Satan

John 8:34   Eph 2 2   2 Tim 2 25.26
Whosoever   ye   Instructing
committeth   walked   that
sin   according to   they may
is the   the spirit that   recover
servant   now worketh   themselves
of   in the   out of the
sin.   children   snare
of   of the devil
disobedience

LESSON VI

FREEDOM

Try to lead the children to Christ as Saviour and Lord.
1. The believer is free from future judgment.
2. The believer is free from present condemnation.

SLAVERY, and especially slavery to sin, self and Satan, is a very unhappy state. But I am not unhappy today, and I do not feel like a slave. I believe I am free. But you might ask me, "How do you know you are free?" If a man came to you and said he felt like a policeman, you would not believe him unless you saw his badge. I have a proof that I am free, though, and I am going to show it to you. When a slave was freed in the old days, he was given "emancipation papers." I have an emancipation paper which you may see. It has a black cover. Do you know what it is? Yes, the Bible. There I find that I am no longer a slave, but free, because I have believed in the Lord Jesus Christ.

Turn in your Bible to John 8:36. There you read, "If the Son (the Lord Jesus) therefore shall make you free, ye shall be free indeed." The Lord Jesus is the one who freed me from sin, by dying on the cross; from self, by dying on the cross; from Satan, by dying on the cross. Everything that he has done for me is written down in the Bible, and my freedom is written there in this verse. Another verse is Gal. 5:1, where Paul wrote to some believers to stand fast in the liberty with which Christ had made them free. Because of these verses, since I believe in the Lord Jesus, I know that Satan is no longer my master, and that the collar and chain of self and sin have been broken off and I am free.

If you should set a black slave free he would not understand at first just what his freedom meant. He might think it meant only that he did not have to be whipped when he did not do enough work. You and I need to know just what our freedom means, too.

First, we are set free from judgment. You know that God has said, "The wages of sin is death." We have "all sinned and come short of the glory of God," so we have all earned those wages, and we deserve to be judged. But Christ died to set us free from that judgment. He took our punishment for us so we would not have to be punished. Before we were saved we were like people in a prison cell, waiting to be sent to the electric chair. We were prisoners of Satan, and we were waiting for judgment, which would send us to hell. But Christ came, and freed us from this. He said we need not be punished; we need not be judged. When the great judgment day comes, not one saved person will be judged. Read John 5: 24. The long word "condemnation" is the same as the word "judgment." Read the verse again with that word instead. It might be a good plan to write the word "judgment" in the margin, so you will remember what the verse means.

Yet a man in a prison cell would not be entirely free, just because he was not to be sent to the electric chair. He would need to be let out of his cell. And God has let us out of the cell of present condemnation. All who do not believe in Jesus are "condemned already" (John 3:18); that is, they are as good as judged even while they are still alive, but we who believe are free from the fear of judgment, and free from God's sentence of "guilty," even now. Rom. 8:1, and John 3:18 are two verses to prove it all to you. Read them at least twice, so you will never forget them.

NOTEBOOK SUGGESTION: Explain that because Christ died for us we are no longer slaves but free. We have been let out of the prison cell of *present condemnation* so that we do not have to be afraid of God's wrath. We are also free from *future judgment*, because Christ took our judgment for us on the cross.

The Prison Cell of Condemnation and Judgment

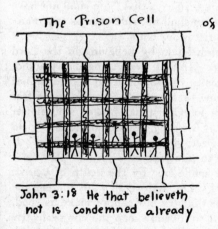

John 3:18 He that believeth not is condemned already

Romans 8 1 There is therefore now no condemnation to them which are in Christ Jesus.

LESSON VII

FREEDOM

Try to lead the children to Christ as Saviour and Lord.
1. We are free from bondage to sin.
2. We are free from the law.

WOULD a man who escaped and ran away from prison be free? He would no longer be behind the bars, and so he would be free in a certain sense, but all the police in the country would be looking for him, and waiting to put him back in prison again. That is not the kind of freedom that we have. Christ has *made* us free, and our old master, Satan, has no right to try to take us back into his slavery again. In our first lesson we said that we were in slavery to three masters—Satan, sin and self. These no longer have any power over us, because Christ is our Saviour.

It is wonderful to know that we are free from sin. That does not mean only that we will not be punished for our sins. It means that our sins have been taken away. Sin was like a heavy burden that we had to carry. Now Christ has taken it all away, and we are free from it. We will prove it from our Bibles. Turn to Rom. 6:18 and 22. Read them carefully and see what they say we are free from. Sin was not only like a burden, it was also like a terrible king ruling over us. But Rom. 6:14 says that "Sin shall not have dominion over you," which means that sin shall not rule over us any more. It can no longer make us obey it, for Christ is our King.

It used to be, before you were born again by believing in the Lord Jesus Christ you could not help sinning. In fact, everything that you did, whether it seemed good or bad, was really sin, for unsaved people cannot do anything that pleases God. But now that you are saved, you are free from sinning—you do not have to sin, for Christ has broken sin's power over you. If you are tempted to do what is wrong, you do not have to yield to the temptation, because Christ has freed you from the power of sin. If you trust in Him, sin will not continue to rule your life.

Another thing from which we are made free by the death of Christ, is the law. Now the law is a very good thing, and we all want to keep the ten commandments. But the trouble is that the law cannot make us good, for we are all sinners, and so weak that we cannot keep the law perfectly. So, instead of making us good, the law just shows us that we are not good.

Try as we may, that is, of course, in our own strength, we find ourselves breaking God's law every day. In Deuteronomy we read the commandment, "Thou shalt love the Lord thy God with all thine heart." Now you know that you do not love God with all your heart, for you often do things that displease Him. So this part of the law makes you unhappy, for it shows you how bad you are. Yet the death of Christ has even freed us from this, for God tells us that we are no longer under the law. (Read Gal. 3:24, 25; Gal. 4:5; Rom. 7:6). This does not mean that we may break the law, but that God's Holy Spirit Who lives in all who are born again, will keep the law for us, so that all we will have to do will be to trust Him, instead of trying, trying, trying, to keep the law. If we yield our hearts to Him, and do as He shows us moment by moment, we will be happy for we will be pleasing our Lord.

NOTEBOOK SUGGESTIONS: Tell the children because Christ died for us, He is our king, and sin no longer rules over us. We do not have to be a slave to sin, any more. We used to be under the law, but now the Holy Spirit lives in us, and we trust Him that He make us both happy and holy. Have the children draw the heart. You should have a model for them to trace around. You should also prepare white paper hearts a little larger than the one drawn to paste over this one when the drawing is complete. Paste only at the top points so that the heart can be lifted up. On the top heart draw the crown and write beneath the words: Christ, not Sin, is King.

Christ, not sin, is King

LESSON VIII

FREEDOM

Try to lead the children to Christ as Saviour and Lord.

1. We are free from fear.
2. We are free from care.

SOMETIMES small boys and girls are very much afraid of the dark. They do not even like to go to bed in the dark. Of course when they are older they become free from that fear. But even older people are afraid of some things. Yet if we belong to the Lord Jesus we need not be afraid of anything, for He has made us free from fear. Read Rom. 8:15. There you find that we are not in bondage or slavery, so that we need to be afraid. And in 1 John 4:18 we find that God's perfect love to us casts out our fear.

Many people are afraid of death and well they may be if they are not saved, for then death means separation from God forever in hell. But even some who have believed in God in the time before Christ died, were afraid of death, because they knew so very little of life beyond the grave. In Heb. 2:15 we read of Christ's delivering those who spent their whole lives in slavery because of fear of death. Fear was like a terrible master who kept them always unhappy and miserable. They were slaves to this fear. But then Christ came, and died, and rose again from the dead, so now there is no fear of death for us. That fear is gone forever. Psa. 23:4 says that we need fear no evil because the Lord is with us. Death only means going home to Heaven for those who are His.

God has planned everything in our lives. Nothing can happen to us unless He lets it, so we do not have to be afraid of what may happen, day or night. If we are sick, we can just rest quietly, knowing that the Lord will do for us what is best. If we have hard lessons in school, we can just ask the Lord to help us with them, and be sure He will, if we do our best, too. We need not be afraid of anything at all, since we belong to God, and He is our Father and loves us and cares for us.

Another enemy that some Christians let be their masters is worry. They worry about everything—about what has happened, about what may happen, and about what may not happen. They are never quiet and content. There is a little verse that speaks of this:

Said the robin to the sparrow, I should really like to know,
Why these anxious human beings rush about and worry so.
Said the sparrow to the robin, Well, I think that it must be
That they have no heavenly Father, such as cares for you and me.

Of course birds cannot talk, nor think about such things, but it is true that we seem to be more worried than they. Yet God cares more for us than for the birds (Matt. 6:26). Read 1 Pet. 5:7, Phil. 4:6 and Matt. 6:25-34 to see what God says about His care for us. He takes care of us; why should we worry? Do we think that He cannot do it well?

So you see all fear is gone. We do not have to worry about slavery any more for we are free from all bad things. We are free from condemnation and judgment, from the power of sin, and from the law and even from fear and worry. We can lift up our heads, and rejoice in all that God has done for us.

NOTEBOOK SUGGESTIONS: For review it would be well to have the class find and write in the notebook a verse to prove each of these points after the pictures are drawn.

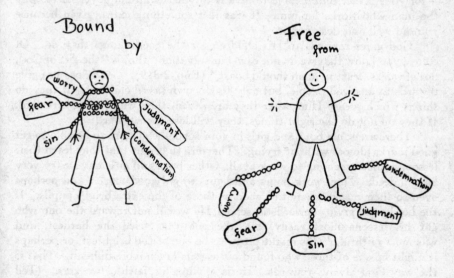

TEST QUESTIONS ON SIN ON PAGE 142.

LESSON IX

SALVATION AND REWARDS

The importance of these lessons lies in the fact that many Christians fail to understand the principle of grace which underlies them. Though they may be sincerely trusting in Christ, many have the mistaken idea that they must do something to merit salvation. If you teach these lessons faithfully, you can remove this error once for all from the minds of your pupils.

Try to lead the children to Christ as Saviour and Lord.
1. What are rewards?
2. The basis of rewards.
3. What will the rewards be?

DID you ever receive a reward? Perhaps your father promised you something that you wanted very much, if your report card were especially good. The good thing that he promised you was not pay —for your father didn't have to give it to you, as an employer has to pay the man who works for him. It was just something extra, given because you did well and deserved it.

God gives rewards to His children for the good things they do. Of course you know that we do not earn our salvation; that is "the gift of God, not of works, lest any man should boast" (Eph. 2:8, 9). God does not give rewards to unsaved people, but only to His own saved children. If they do things which please Him, after they are saved, they will receive a reward. If they do not do the right things, they will lose their reward.

There are some boys and girls in your school who seem to be able to get good marks almost without trying. They are so bright that they learn their lessons without seeming to work at all. Other boys and girls have to try very hard indeed. They work hours and hours to get good marks, and perhaps even so their marks are not so good as those of the extra bright pupils. If the Lord were giving rewards in school, He would not reward the one who got his lessons most easily, but the one who tried the hardest, and was most faithful. This might prove to be one of the brightest, or perhaps it might be one of those who found his lessons much more difficult. That is the way God always rewards. He is looking for faithful workers. (Tell the parable of Matt. 25:14-30, noting that the reward to the man who had two talents and to the man who had five, was exactly the same—vs. 21 and

23 are identical).   Rev. 2:10b promises a crown to the one who is faithful. Any one of us can win a reward, then, if we will only be faithful.

God's word tells of a number of things for which we can receive a reward.
(Look up and discuss the following references: Matt. 10:41, 42; Matt. 5:
11, 12; Dan. 12:3; 2 Tim. 4:8; James 1:12; Col. 3:23, 24; 1 Cor. 9:24, 25).

We do not know just what these rewards will be. The verses we have
read speak of rewards, and crowns, and "shining."   Shall we have real gold
crowns, with precious stones in them? We do not know. This may be in
Heaven's language a symbol of some great blessing, which we could not
even understand in earth's language. But whatever these rewards are, they
will be very wonderful indeed, and we shall be very happy to have them.

The very best thing about these rewards is that it will make the Lord
Jesus happy if He can give them to us. He wants us to have them, and He
will be even happier than we are when we receive them.

We can have these rewards if we are faithful every day, and let the
Lord Jesus rule in our lives. "Trust and obey" should be our motto. If
we do that, we may be sure of having rewards when the Lord Jesus gives
them out.

NOTEBOOK SUGGESTIONS: Let the children choose one of the verses in the lesson to write
    out beneath the picture.

We sow
our seed
here

We get our
reward in
Heaven

LESSON X

SALVATION AND REWARDS

Try to lead the children to Christ as Saviour and Lord.
The contrast between salvation and rewards:
1. Salvation is free.
2. Rewards are earned.
3. Salvation is a present possession.
4. Rewards are a future attainment.

THERE is a great difference between salvation and rewards, and it is just there that some Christian people get mixed. You boys and girls can understand from this lesson what it takes some people many years to learn. There are two great differences between salvation and rewards. The first is that salvation is free, and rewards are earned; the second that salvation is obtained now and that rewards are for the future.

You cannot do anything to deserve salvation. You could work all your life long, and yet you could not earn it. The only way to be saved is to believe in the Lord Jesus Christ (Acts 16:31; John 3:16). Over and over in the Bible we read that salvation is a *gift* (Rom. 6:23; Eph. 2:8, 9). If I gave you a nice Christmas present, you would not come to me and say, "Thank you for the gift. I have brought you a pound to pay for it." If you paid for it, it would not be a gift any more. So you cannot pay for salvation. It is a gift, and if you tried to pay for it, it would not be a gift any more. All you can do is just to receive salvation freely. It is "not of works" (Eph. 2:9). You are saved by what the Lord Jesus did when He died on the cross, not by anything that you can ever do.

Rewards are just the opposite of salvation. They are not a gift, but must be earned. Christians, that is, those who have been saved, may earn the rewards by the work they do for the Lord. Every time the Bible speaks of rewards it shows that the rewards are given for doing something. Do you remember some of those things?

So we can surely tell the difference between salvation and rewards in this, that salvation is a free gift, and that rewards are always earned by good works.

The other great difference between the two is that we have one of them now, but must wait till we get to Heaven for the other one. Which one do we have now? Salvation, of course. There are many verses that show that we *have* eternal life right now. (Look up 1 John 5:11; 2 Pet. 1:3; Titus 3:4, 5; 2 Tim. 1:9; John 3:36; John 5:24; John 6:47). Because we have eternal life *now*, we can say that we *are saved*, not that we will be saved when we get to Heaven.

Our rewards we cannot have until we get to Heaven. They will be waiting for us then. Note that every one of the verses that speaks of rewards speaks of the future. It is not that we *have* rewards now, but we *shall have* them in the future. The verses speak of receiving rewards in Heaven, too, and that is not now, as we very well know! (Read the following verses to see the future in each one: Matt. 10:41, 42; Col. 3:22-24; Matt. 5:11, 12; Dan. 12:3; 2 Tim. 4:8.)

It is wonderful that we have our salvation now. It makes us very happy to know that we are saved, and càn never be lost. And we can look forward happily, too, to the time when God will distribute the rewards to us in Heaven. What a day of rejoicing that will be if we have been faithful and have earned rewards which we can receive at that great day. We must be diligent now, however, and never forget that it is in these days that we earn the rewards. When we get to Heaven it will be too late.

NOTEBOOK SUGGESTION: Have the children choose a verse to write beneath the illustration.

LESSON XI

SALVATION AND REWARDS

Try to lead the children to Christ as Saviour and Lord.

1. When are rewards received?
2. What is the purpose of rewards?

W E KNOW that we shall not receive our rewards now, but at some future time, for that was in our last lesson. But just when will this time of rewarding be? The Bible gives us the answer to this question.

We are expecting our Lord Jesus Christ to return at any moment. When He comes, all those who died believing in Him will be raised from the dead and given beautiful bodies like the body of the Lord Jesus. At the same time those believers who are still alive, will be changed. Their bodies will be made like that of Lord Jesus, too. (Read 1 Thess. 4:13-18, 1 Cor. 15:51, 52, and 1 John 3:2, and show that these truths are to be found in those verses.) It will be then, when the dead in Christ have been raised, and the living changed and caught up into the air to meet the Lord, that God will look at our records to see whether or not we shall deserve a reward. Read Matt. 16:27. Luke 14:13, 14 are the words of the Lord Jesus. He told His followers to be kind to the poor and the sick and crippled, and they should be recompensed, or rewarded, when? At the resurrection of the just. And when is it that the just, or the believers in Christ, are raised? It is when Christ comes again. So we can see clearly that the rewards will be given when the Lord Jesus comes. Then the books will be opned, a nd God will review the history of our lives. The sins have been blotted out, for Jesus died to do that. But the record will show a list of our good works,— or, if we have not been faithful and done the good works that we should, there will be a great blank space. What a sad thing that would be, for that would mean that we would not receive any rewards.

Why does God say He will reward those who are faithful? I think we can guess. Why does father sometimes offer you a reward if you have a fine report? It is because he is eager to have you try hard. He wants to encourage you. Just so God is eager to have you try hard to do good works, and wants to encourage you. Of course we ought to do right, just because it is right, and because we know God desires it, but our Heavenly Father knows us very well, and He sees that if He offers us rewards, it will help us and encourage us.

In Matt. 5:11, 12 the Lord spoke to those who would have great trials and persecutions. He encouraged them by telling them that their reward for bearing this persecution would be great in Heaven. Read over the promises of rewards and see how each one encourages us to be faithful and earnest in our work for the Lord. (The teacher can make a list of the references from the foregoing lessons, and present them at this time.)

Think about the great rewards that God has promised, and see if it does not help you to be more faithful. Anything that you do well, whether it is your school work, or your work at home, or anything at all, if you do it for Jesus' sake, deserves a reward. Even a cup of cold water given to some one, because you want to please Jesus, will receive a reward in Heaven.

NOTEBOOK SUGGESTION: Explain the diagram to the children as they draw.

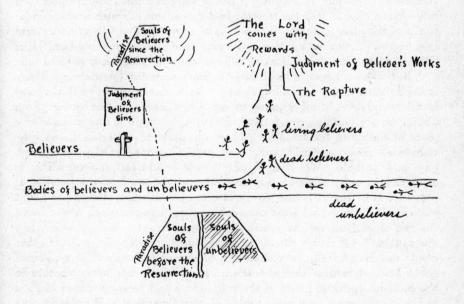

LESSON XII

SALVATION AND REWARDS

This lesson is a little different from most, for it is a study of a passage of Scripture, not a gathering of many passages on a given subject. Be sure the children have their Bibles (they should always have them, of course). Show them that the purpose is to find out just what the passage means.

Try to lead the children to Christ as Saviour and Lord.

OUR study today is going to be of five verses in 1 Cor. 3. They are verses about rewards, and in this passage God tells us just what we need to know. We will study the verses one by one to learn just what they mean.

First let us read the verses all together—1 Cor. 3:11-15.

Verse 11 is a verse about salvation. It speaks of the foundation of our faith. What is a foundation? The foundation of a house is the firm structure upon which it is built. A house without a foundation would soon fall. Matt. 7:24-27 tells the story of two houses, one of which had a foundation and the other did not. The one with no foundation fell, when a storm came up on it. Our foundation is the only true foundation—the Lord Jesus Christ. He is the one in whom we believe, and who keeps us saved and safe.

But when a house is built there is more than the foundation. There is the building on top of the foundation. Verse eleven speaks of this. Jesus is the foundation, the beginning of our Christian life. But as we go on living, we are building every day. Everything we do is like a stone or a piece of timber in the building. There are different materials that Christians use. Some use gold, silver and precious stones. Others use wood, hay and stubble. Which kind of building would last longer? This is explained in verse twelve. But verse thirteen shows how the building is proved. This time it is not with a storm, but with fire—the fire of God's justice. If a fire should start near one of these houses, which would burn, the one of gold, silver and precious stones, or the one made of wood, hay and stubble? Of course the latter would burn immediately, but the other would not burn at all, for you cannot set fire to a diamond, or a piece of gold! The judgment of the believer's works will show right away whether he has built his spiritual house of the gold, silver and precious stones of good works, or the wood, hay and stubble of worthless deeds. We should note that "any man" does not mean every man, but any believer. If a teacher says, "Any boy may have one of these books," he does not mean any boy in town, but any boy in the class.

Verse fourteen brings us back to the subject we have been studying—rewards. For it tells us what? That if any believer's work remains, and is not burned, which he has built on the one true foundation of faith in Christ, he will receive a reward. That is exactly what we have learned. At that day when Jesus comes and we come before Him to be judged for our works, He will try them, and if they are good, like gold, silver and precious stones, we shall receive a reward.

But verse fifteen gives the darker side of the picture. For there are some who will not trust and obey the Lord. They would rather have their own way, even though they are saved. They like to choose their own works, and too often they are not good works, but works of wood, hay and stubble. When the fire of judgment (the fire is a symbol of the searching of the Lord into our works) comes, these works prove to be no good, and are "burned," or judged to be worthless. Then he "suffers loss"—which means that he loses his reward. But, since he is a saved man, he does not lose his salvation, but only his reward. He himself is saved, yet so as by fire, or as though he had been saved from a burning house—just himself saved, but not a single thing with him. Surely we want to build with gold, silver and precious stones, so that we will be like the first man, and not like the one who loses his possessions.

NOTEBOOK SUGGESTION: Give the class the symbols and see if they can supply the explanation of them in the verses they have just studied.

= Foundation = Jesus Christ the Lord

= Building = Our Christian lives

= Gold, silver, precious stones = good works (Eph 2:10)

= Wood, hay, stubble = works of the flesh

= fire = judgment

TEST QUESTIONS ON SALVATION AND REWARDS ON PAGE 142.

LESSON XIII

THINGS TO COME

Try to lead the children to Christ as Saviour and Lord.

1. Not all the world is to be converted.
2. The apostasy.

IT WOULD be foolish to try to do something that God says will not be done, wouldn't it? Yet some Christians are working very hard, hoping to bring in the millenium by converting the whole world. Do you know what the millenium is? It is that wonderful time described in the Bible, when Christ will reign here, and all then living in the world will be under His rule. Yet in spite of all the good work Christians may do, they cannot bring everyone to Christ.

What was the Lord Jesus' last command to His disciples? He told them to go into all the world and preach the Gospel to every creature (Matt. 28:19). That is a command to us, too. We are obeying Him if we are doing everything we can to bring people to the Lord Jesus. We can be witnesses (Acts 1:8) telling them what Christ has done for us, and how He has saved us and wants to save them too, but we must not think that *we* can convert them. Only God can give eternal life to people. And we must not think, either, that everybody is going to be converted, for God's Word tells us distinctly that many will refuse to believe in Christ. (John 3: 19; 1 Cor. 1:26; Matt. 13:1-23—this is the parable of the sower, and shows that only part of the seed sown bears fruit. You will have to explain the symbols carefully, leaving nothing to the imagination of the children, for symbols are not too easy to understand.)

Today God is forming the Church. By that we do not mean building church buildings, but saving those who believe in the Lord Jesus Christ and making them part of that great group of believers which God's Word calls "*The* Church." There are many churches, but only one great Church, to which all those who are born again belong. It is not Presbyterian, or Catholic or Angelican, but includes all from all denominations who have truly been born again by believing in the Lord Jesus Christ. This will not include everybody in the whole world, but there will be some from every nation. When the very last person whom God has chosen to be a part of this Church has been saved, then the Lord Jesus will come again.

In the Bible we read some sad things about the time before the Lord shall come. We are told that before He comes there will be an *apostasy*. Do you know what that word means? Apostasy is going away from the true faith. When the Bible tells us that there will be an apostasy before Christ comes, it means that many people will refuse to believe the truth and turn to lies. This will even happen in the church—not the true Church, of course, among those who are really born again, but in the churches. That is true today. Many ministers in churches that are supposed to be all right, are preaching things that are not in the Bible, and even saying that the Bible is not true (2 Tim. 3:1-5; 2 Tim. 4:3, 4; 2 Pet. 2:1, 2). Since there is a great apostasy even now, we know that the Lord Jesus may come back very soon, and we look forward with joy to seeing Him. In the meantime, we must ask Him to keep us faithful, and not let us be influenced by those who are preaching and teaching lies, because of the apostasy.

NOTEBOOK SUGGESTIONS: Explain the following diagram thus, as they draw: The world is going down, down, away from God. But God is calling out one here, another there, to be His own. When they believe, they are born again, and made a part of The Church.

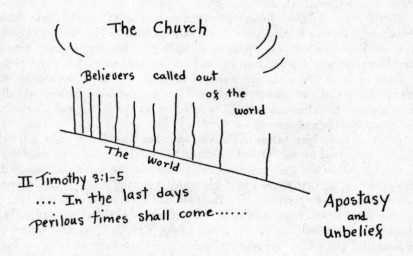

LESSON XIV

THINGS TO COME

1. The rapture.
2. The judgment of believers.
3. The marriage supper.

WHEN the moment comes that God has decided upon, the Lord
Jesus is going to come again. We do not know when it will be,
but it may be any time—even today. Jesus tells us to watch for
His coming (Matt. 25:13). Suddenly there will be a shout, which we shall
hear, and the voice of the archangel and the trump of God. Then those
who have been believers and have died, will be raised from the dead, and
will have beautiful strong bodies like the Lord Jesus'. Believers who are
still alive will be changed so that they will be like Jesus too (1 John 3:2;
Phil. 3:20, 21), and they will be caught up together with those who have been
raised from the dead to meet the Lord in the air. (Read 1 Thess. 4:13-17;
this would be a good passage to have the class attempt to explain phrase by
phrase; also 1 Cor. 15:51, 52.)

At this time the Lord Jesus will not come all the way to the earth, but
we shall meet Him in the air, and He will take us back to Heaven with Him.
Have you ever seen a magnet pick up a needle? When the magnet comes
near, the needle will hop right up to meet it. But the magnet will not pick
up pieces of wood. So when Jesus comes, all who are Christians will go to
meet Him, but those who are not saved will not go, any more than wood will
rise to a magnet. The unsaved will be left here on the earth, and they will
have much trouble and sorrow.

After we have been taken to Heaven with the Lord Jesus, there will be
a time of judgment for us. Only Christians will be there, and of course they
will not be judged for their sin, for Christ died for their sins, and washed
them all away, so that there is not even any record of the sins any more.
They are forgiven, forgotten, gone. But God does have a record of our works
after we have been saved, and it is about these works that we are to be
judged. Have we built our life with good works (Eph. 2:10) which are strong
and beautiful like gold, silver and precious stones? Or have we built our life
with poor works that are weak, and not pleasing to God like wood, hay
and stubble (1 Cor. 3:12, 13)? The judgment will try our works, just as

fire would show the difference between gold, silver and precious stones, wood, hay and stubble. God knows whether we have tried to please Him or not. If our works have been good, we shall receive a reward at this judgment (1 Cor. 3:14) but if they have not been good, if we have been lazy and disobedient Christians, we shall lose our reward, even though we ourselves shall be saved, yet it will be as though we had just barely been saved from a burning house, without a thing to take with us (1 Cor. 3:15).

Then there is going to be a great time of rejoicing in Heaven. Those who have rewards will be glad to lay them down before the Lord Jesus. Those who did not receive a reward will be thankful that they are saved at all. Then there is to be a great feast, called the marriage feast of the Lamb, the Lord Jesus. When your mother and father loved each other very much they were married so that they could always be together. So the Lord Jesus always wishes to be with His own people, His Church. He is called the Bridegroom, and the Church, (all the believers,) is called the Bride. There will be great joy, and from that time on we shall never, never be separated from the Lord Jesus again (Rev. 19:7, 8; 1 Thess. 4:18).

NOTEBOOK SUGGESTIONS: This outline should become very familiar to all the children. It will be as they continue to draw it; be sure you let them know you expect them to become familiar with it by their frequent drawing of it. Do not try to make them commit it to memory; encourage them rather to remember as they draw it so that they will remember without effort.

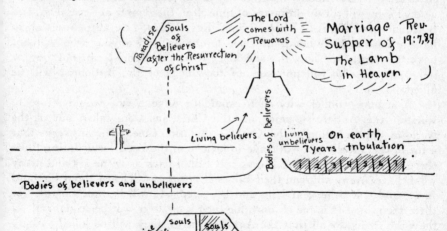

LESSON XV

THINGS TO COME

1. The tribulation.
2. The Antichrist.
3. The tribulation believers.
4. Armageddon.

WHEN believers have been raised from the dead, or taken up from the earth in changed bodies like the Lord Jesus', there will be left here only those who are not Christians. Can you imagine what the world will be like on the day when the Lord comes? Some boys and girls will have disappeared from school. Some shopkeepers, bankers, bus conductors, and ministers and mothers and fathers will be gone. There will be great fear in the hearts of many of the unbelievers who are left behind, surely.

For a while all may seem to go well. A great man will come with plans for the governments of the world, and everyone will think that he is wonderful. He will become ruler over much of the world. But though he will seem so fine and so kind, his heart belongs to Satan, for he will be the Antichrist. After about three years he will begin to show his true character, for he will set up an image of himself in the temple at Jerusalem, and make men worship it (2 Thess. 2:3, 4; Rev. 13:15). He also causes all to have a mark in their hands or their foreheads, and anyone who will not have this mark, to show his allegiance to the Antichrist can not buy or sell. Anyone who will not worship the image of the Antichrist will be killed.

You may wonder why there would be anyone who would refuse to worship the Antichrist, since all the Christians were taken out of the world at the beginning of this Great Tribulation time. The answer is that some of the unbelievers will come to believe in the Lord Jesus during those three years. God will send Moses and Elijah back as witnesses and many will believe. Many will read their Bibles. There they will learn about the Lord Jesus, and will believe in Him and be saved. It will be much harder for them then, than it is for us now, for their very lives will be in danger. If they refuse to do all that the Antichrist says, they will be killed. Many of them will be martyred, or killed for Jesus' sake. Rev. 14:13 and 6:9, 10 speak of these. Many of the Jews will go throughout the world preaching about Jesus.

Great judgments will be poured out by God upon the earth, for this is a time of wrath. The unbelievers will have trouble and tribulation such as we never could imagine. There will be earthquakes, and famine and war and disease. And still these unbelieving people, many, many of them, will refuse to turn to the Lord. They will be stubborn in their unbelief.

At last, near the end of this Great Tribulation, there will be a great war, in which all the world will fight. All will be on one side or the other. We do not know how long the war will last, but it will be a terrible one. The last great battle is called the battle of Armageddon. It is described in Rev. 16:14-16, and 19:17-19. It will be a horrible battle but it will be stopped in the middle, for the Lord Jesus Himself will stop it. He will come as is described in Rev. 19:11-16, and will put an end to this battle. Then the Great Tribulation will be ended. The nations that have disobeyed the Lord will be judged, and punished, and He will set up His Kingdom here on the earth.

NOTEBOOK SUGGESTION: Same as last week.

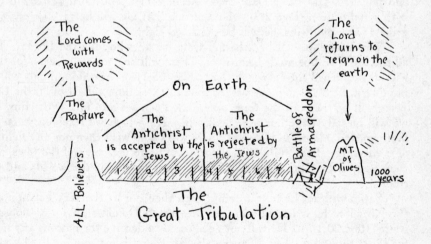

LESSON XVI

THINGS TO COME

1. The setting up of the Kingdom.
2. The character of the Kingdom.
3. The liberation of Satan.
4. The final judgment and eternal state.

AFTER the Tribulation, in the Battle of Armageddon, Christ is going to return to the earth. When He came for believers, you remember, He met them in the air. Now He returns to the earth, and His feet shall stand on the Mount of Olives (Zech. 14:1-4). He will take the Antichrist captive, and will cast him, and those who worshipped his image into the lake of fire (Rev. 19:20). Then He will set up His Kingdom here on earth.

That will be a very wonderful Kingdom, and it will be set up by the power of God. The Lord Jesus will not be meek and lowly then, but glorious and powerful (Isa. 9:7; Dan. 2:44; Zech. 2:11). The Lord Jesus will rule with a rod of iron (Psa. 2:9), which means that He will be very severe with evil. If any man sins, he will be punished right away.

The Kingdom will be a happy time for all who love the Lord. Then all the world will be made beautiful. There will be no more deserts, for they will all be turned into gardens (Isa. 51:3; 35:1). The wild animals will be tame (Isa. 11:6-9). No one will be hurt in those days. Best of all the Lord Jesus will be there all the time, where men can see and talk with Him, but we will already have our new bodies like His which we received when He first came to take us to Heaven. There will be no wars then nor any fighting or quarreling. The capitol of the world will be Jerusalem, and the Jews, who then will all be Christians, will be the chief people of the world, and the rulers.

Satan will not be free to tempt men then, for at the very beginning of the Kingdom he is bound and cast into the bottomless pit for a thousand years (Rev. 20:1-3). He will not be allowed to deceive the nations any more for those thousand years. During the Kingdom, when anyone does wrong, it will be wholly his own fault, for he will not be tempted by Satan. There will be wrongdoing, for men will still be sinners, but the Lord will always punish immediately, and there will not be crime and sinning to the extent that there is today.

At the end of the thousand years, God is going to give one final test to men. He allows Satan to come out of his prison house for a little time (Rev. 20:7). Immediately he will go out to tempt and deceive people and try to gather them together against the Lord. Men's hearts are so bad that even after a thousand years of righteousness on the earth, they will be tired of what is good, and will join Satan against the Lord. But when they gather together to fight against the Lord and those who are His, God will destroy them (Rev. 20:8, 9).

Then comes the last great judgment. Satan is cast into the lake of fire where the Antichrist already has been for a thousand years. A great white throne of judgment will be set up, and all the dead—those who have died without believing in the Lord Jesus Christ, beginning way back with Cain, the first unbeliever, will be brought before God for judgment. None of the believers will be judged, for Christ bore their judgment at the cross. All those whose names were not in the Lamb's book of life will be judged, according to their works, and they will be cast into hell with Satan. The saved will be in Heaven with God for eternity.

NOTEBOOK SUGGESTION: Same as last week.

TEST QUESTIONS ON THINGS TO COME ON PAGE 143.

LESSON XVII

SATAN

Try to lead the children to Christ as Saviour and Lord.
1. Satan's origin.
2. His fall.

GOD did not create Satan as he is now, for certainly Satan is very bad indeed. Where did Satan come from then? Surely he could not make himself, and besides we know that God created all things. The answer is that Satan was not always what he is now. When he was made by God he was like everything else that God ever made—perfect and good.

In Ezek. 28, beginning with the twelfth verse, we find a description of this being as he was when God made him, "full of wisdom, perfect in beauty." In the next verse we find that every precious stone was his covering,—this may refer to the palace in which he lived, or to his clothing. Evidently he was a master of music, for it speaks of "tabrets and pipes." God says too (v. 14) that he was the anointed cherub, which means that he had a very high place in God's kingdom. It seems that he was the highest of all the angels and ruled over all of them for God. His name was Lucifer, we find in Isa. 14:12, and he was called "the son of the morning." Lucifer means "light-bearer," or "day-star," and is a very beautiful name. Yet the wonderful angel who bore this name became our worst enemy.

Isa. 14:13-15 tells us how it happened. The angel who had always worshipped God and ruled the universe for Him ceased thinking how wonderful God was, and began to think of himself. His heart was lifted up because of his beauty (Ezek. 28:17). Probably he thought how nice it would be if all those angels who had been worshipping God so faithfully would worship him instead. The moment that these thoughts entered his heart he had sinned, and this was the very first sin that was ever committed. Before, everyone had been perfect. Man had not yet been made, and all the angels were sinless. Of course God was absolutely perfect. So, with Lucifer's pride the first sin entered the universe. Do you wonder that God particularly hates the sin of pride?

In Isaiah we read what Lucifer said: "I will ascend into Heaven; I will exalt my throne above the clouds . . . I will be like the Most High." Lucifer wanted to take God's place! He would have been glad to put God off His throne, and to have taken it for himself. Of course he could not do it, but the sin of wishing to was there just the same.

Of course after he had sinned, he could not keep on ruling for God. He lost his beautiful name and became the Devil, or Satan. He could not live in Heaven with God, but was cast out. The Lord Jesus, in Luke 10:18 said He saw Satan fall like lightning from Heaven. God did not take away all his power, for he is not chained today, but goes about doing his evil work. Many people belong to him, and belong to his kingdom, instead of to the kingdom of God. He hates God and hates all those who belong to God. In fact he does not even love those who belong to him, but does them all the harm he can.

It is a sad story, for sin always makes sadness. But it explains to us where Satan came from and where sin began. We are glad to know that Jesus conquered Satan when He died on the cross, and that someday all his evil work will be over, and he will be put out of the way forever and ever.

NOTEBOOK SUGGESTIONS: Bring cardboard circles to class so that the children can have them to trace around. Emphasize that there may be millions of years between verses one and two of Genesis, and that we have no idea how long the chaotic condition of verse two lasted.

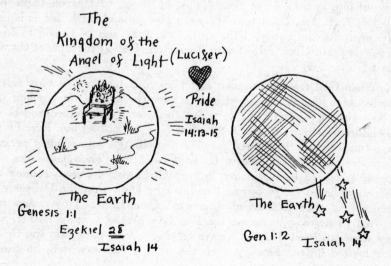

The
Kingdom of the
Angel of Light (Lucifer)

Pride
Isaiah
14:13-15

The Earth
Genesis 1:1
Ezekiel 25
Isaiah 14

The Earth
Gen 1:2   Isaiah 14

LESSON XVIII

SATAN

Try to lead the children to Christ as Saviour and Lord.

1. Satan's personality.
2. His work in history.

DO YOU know what a person is? You have seen a great many persons, but not all are alike. God is a person, yet He is very different from human persons. He does not have a body as we do. Those who have died and gone to Heaven are persons, yet they do not now have bodies. A person is one who can think, and feel, and will, or decide to do things.

Satan is a person, though he is not like us. He is not human, but he can think, and feel and decide, so he is a person. Isa. 14:13 says that he "said in his heart"—that is thinking. Rev. 12:12 speaks of his having great wrath—that is a feeling. And in Isa. 14:13, 14, he says "I will" several times. That is deciding. So he has all the qualities of a person. He is not just some kind of thing, but a person with great wisdom (Ezek. 28:12).

Satan is not in hell, and has never been there, though God will one day put him in the lake of fire. He is, at times, in Heaven (Eph. 6:12; Job 1:6; Zech. 3:1, 2), at times between Heaven and earth, for he is called "the prince of the power of the air" (Eph. 2:2), and he is said to have a throne on earth (Rev. 2:13) and will have one here at the time of the Antichrist (Rev. 13:2).

When God created the man and woman, Satan wanted to have them worship him just as he had wished to have the angels worship him when he first sinned. So he came to tempt them, and they sinned and became his children (Gen. 3; 1 John 3:10). But God did not let him have his own way, and keep all the human race for himself. He immediately promised a Deliverer Who should destroy Satan (Gen. 3:15). Then Satan was angry indeed, and tried in every way to keep God's promise from coming true. He always hated God's people Israel, for he knew that the Deliverer was promised as a descendent of Abraham (Gen. 12:3). How many times he tried to destroy them—at the Red Sea, at the time of Esther, when they were captives! He was always seeking to lead them into sin, through their wicked kings. Finally, when the baby Jesus was born, he tried to destroy Him (Matt. 2:16-18). Then in Matt. 4 he tried to tempt Him to sin, for if he could have done that, He could never have been the Redeemer. (Tell these stories as graphically as possible.) Another time he stirred up the people to try to kill Jesus (Luke 4:28-30), and still again raised a great storm at sea to try to drown Him (Mark 4:35-41). But none of these attempts were successful, for God has much more power than Satan, and what He says always comes to pass.

Finally, Satan stirred up the chief priests and Pharisees and the people to crucify Jesus. God allowed him to do this, for this was His plan of redemption. Satan did not know it, but he was really doing just what had to be done, in order for Jesus to save us. This was the time which God has spoken of in Genesis 3:15—"He shall bruise thine head, but thou shalt bruise His heel." Satan did do harm to the Lord Jesus, but not irremediable harm, for Christ was not under his power, and after He had suffered and died, He rose again. But Satan was mortally wounded—his head was bruised—for his power was really destroyed there at the cross. Now he cannot touch God's own, and before long he will be cast out entirely.

NOTEBOOK SUGGESTIONS: Explain that Satan, being a spirit, has access to all three abodes, but that he will ultimately be confined to one.

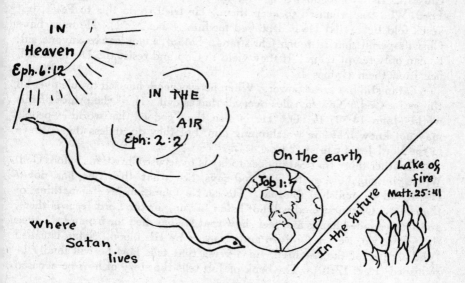

LESSON XIX

SATAN

Try to lead the children to Christ as Saviour and Lord.

1. Satan's work today.
2. His helpers.

THOUGH the Lord Jesus Christ caused the destruction of Satan when He died on the cross, Satan is still free, and still has much power. He is like a criminal who has been pronounced guilty, but not executed yet. What is he doing today?

His chief interest is in keeping unbelievers from being saved. He does everything he can to keep them from believing in the Lord Jesus Christ. Sometimes he blinds their minds, to keep them from understanding the Gospel (2 Cor. 4:3, 4). Sometimes he seems like an angel of light (2 Cor. 11:14), but it is only in order to deceive men. He hates all believers, too, and tries to make them sin, for he knows this will grieve the Lord Jesus (Acts 5:3—the story might well be briefly told—1 Pet. 5:8). Sometimes he causes Christians to do wrong, but he cannot take them away from the Lord, Who has promised to keep them. He tried to do this to Peter, but Jesus told Peter that He had prayed for him (Luke 22:31). He must have Christ's permission to touch Christians. Satan cannot *make* anyone sin; he can only tempt them. If they yield to God and resist the Devil, he will flee from them (James 4:7).

Satan still has great power. When he was good, he used to rule over all things for God. Now he rules over all that is evil. He is the prince of this world (John 14:30; 16:11). He is also the "god of this world"—people may not know they are worshipping him, but they do, unless they believe in the Lord Jesus Christ (2 Cor. 4:4).

Another thing that Satan does today is to accuse Christians before God. When you sin, he goes to God and says, See what that one has done? He should be punished for that. He isn't a Christian—or something of that kind. Of course God will not listen to him, for the Lord Jesus is there, and His wounded hands and feet show that He has died for us, and so, even though we sin, we are forgiven and cleansed by His blood. Satan is called "the accuser of the brethren" in a verse that tells how he will finally be punished (Rev. 12:10). The book of Job tells the story of how he accused that good man before God, saying that if his property, and his health were taken away, he would curse God. That was a lie. Satan is a liar, and the father of lies (John 8:44).

There is only one Devil, but he has many helpers. Not only do wicked men help him, but he has another kind of helper as well. They are wicked spirits called demons. When the Bible speaks of "devils" it is the demons who are meant. These wicked spirits entered into people, possessing them, and making them very wicked and sometimes making them sick. Jesus always helped such people by casting out the demons, who could not have any victory over men when He was there. Since Christ has given us the Holy Spirit, Satan cannot have any victory over us, if we fight in God's way. In the Gospels we often read of those who were possessed of demons. We have to fight a spiritual battle with Satan and his helpers (Eph. 6: 12), but we are sure of the victory if we put on the armour of God (Eph. 6:13-17). And we must never forget that Christ has said, "Greater is He that is in you than he that is in the world" (1 John 4:4).

NOTEBOOK SUGGESTIONS: As the children draw, explain to them that it is very difficult to make any presentation of a spiritual being such as Satan. Much modern error concerning the personality of Satan has arisen from the medieval artist's conception of him as a being with horns, tail, cloven hoofs and a pitchfork. In thus picturing him in the form of a serpent, we merely present one phase of his personality, venomous and treacherous. We must also remember that he is an angel of light. Emphasize the truth of 1 John 4:4.

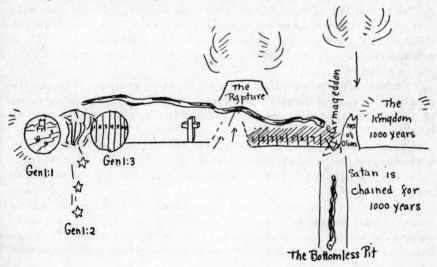

LESSON XX

SATAN

Try to lead the children to Christ as Saviour and Lord.

1. Satan's future.

BEFORE Satan is finally cast into eternal punishment, he is going to make one moᵣe great try to secure all this earth and its kingdoms for himself. He is going to send a man to help in this work, who will be a very powerful servant of his.

We know that sometime, and we believe it will be soon, the Lord Jesus is going to return to take all believers out of the world. Then will come that sorrowful time of judgment called the "Great Tribulation." Before the middle of that time Satan will no longer be allowed to accuse believers before God. He will be cast out of Heaven, where he now accuses us (Rev. 12:7-12). Then he begins his greatest work on earth. He chooses a man, whom God calls the Antichrist, to be a mighty ruler in the earth. To this man he gives great power, and causes people to worship him. This man will do terrible things, finally setting up his own image in the temple at Jerusalem, and causing everybody to worship him. This is Satan's same old trick, you see, of trying to get people to worship him. This was his first sin, and this is what he has wanted ever since. Everyone who will not worship him, for some will be saved even in that terrible time, and will refuse to worship the Antichrist, will be in danger of being killed. Many will be killed.

Finally, after seven years, there will be a great division among the people and nations of the earth, and a great war will be fought. In the midst of the fiercest battle, the Lord Jesus will come back again, and will stop the battle, and cast the Antichrist into the lake of fire.

Then comes Satan's punishment. He will be bound and cast into the bottomless pit, too, for a thousand years (Rev. 20:2). During that thousand years the Lord Jesus will rule on this earth, and Satan will not be able to tempt anyone at all.

But at the end of the thousand years, Satan will be loosed for a little while. Then, because he is very angry, he goes out into all the earth, to deceive the nations, and gather people together to fight against the Lord. Strange as it may seem, men's hearts are so incurably bad, that though they have been living for a thousand years under the reign of the Lord Jesus, a great many of them will join Satan in this terrible battle (Rev. 20:7, 8).

Of course there could be but one end to a battle of that kind. Satan could never win. He has never won a battle yet, though he may seem, for a little while, to be conquering. The end of this battle comes very suddenly. It is described in Rev. 20:9.

Then will come the final punishment of Satan. It is described in just one verse, but it is a punishment that will last forever and ever. He will be cast into the lake of fire—for ever. It is a terrible end to a terrible story, but we can see that God is just in thus punishing the one who brought sin upon the earth.

NOTEBOOK SUGGESTION: Be sure you understand the diagram and then be sure the children do.

I Thess 4: 13-18
The rapture

believers | 1 | 2 | 3 | 4 | 5 | 6 | 7 |

Battle of Armageddon

MT. OF OLIVES

The Millenium
Christ is King

Judgment
of the
Great White
Throne

The seven years
of the rule of
the Antichrist
who is Satan
"in the flesh."
Rev. 12: 7-12

Satan is
bound for
1000 years

Unbelievers
and
fallen angels
are cast
into

The
Lake
of
Fire

TEST QUESTIONS ON SATAN ON PAGE 143.

TEXT QUESTIONS—COURSE THREE

THE BIBLE

1. What two things may be known of God apart from the Bible?
2. Why did God have to give the Bible in addition to nature?
3. What great questions about which men argue are fully answered in the Bible?
4. What does inspiration mean?
5. Quote 2 Peter 1:21.
6. Did the writers of the Bible understand what they were writing?
7. What is the Bible in ten words?
8. How can we understand the Bible?
9. Name five things the Bible is like.
10. Name three things the Bible will do for Christians.

FREEDOM

1. To what three things is an unbeliever in bondage?
2. What did the colored mammy say about Satan?
3. Name four of the things the believer is set free from.
4. What is in the hearts of those where Christ is not King?
5. Can the Lord Jesus set you free from all your fears? Have you ever let him do so? When?
6. Do we become free from sin when we struggle against it?
7. Do Christians have to be ruled by sin?
8. Is Satan the master of all who are slaves to sin?
9. Did the Lord Jesus make us free from sin by His life or by His death?
10. Who is the Master of those set free from sin?

SALVATION AND REWARDS

1. Will unsaved people receive any rewards from God?
2. Will very gifted Christians receive greater rewards than those who are not so gifted? Why?
3. What will be the rewards that God is going to give?
4. Name at least five things for which we may receive rewards.

5. Which do we receive free, salvation or rewards? Or both?
6. What can we do to *earn* salvation?
7. When do we receive our rewards?
8. (a) When do we receive our salvation?
   (b) If we have truly been "born again" is it possible to lose our salvation?
9. Why does God offer rewards to Christians?
10. Explain 1 Cor. 3:15, so that a person who knew nothing about salvation and rewards, would understand it. (The pupils may have a Bible open before them.)

THINGS TO COME

1. Is the whole world going to be converted before Jesus comes?
2. What do we mean by *The* Church?
3. Tell what will happen when Christ comes to believers who have died?
4. What will happen to living believers when Christ comes?
5. The Bible says there will be an apostasy before Jesus comes. What does that mean?
6. Tell what you know about the judgment of believers.
7. What will happen to unbelievers when Jesus comes to take away the believers?
8. Tell all that you know about what kind of person the Antichrist will be?
9. What will happen at the end of the Great Tribulation?
10. Write what you know about the Kingdom, and about what happens at the end of the thousand years.

SATAN

1. Tell something of Lucifer before he fell.
2. What was Lucifer's sin?
3. How do you know Satan is a person?
4. Where is Satan now?
5. Tell the story of how Satan tempted Adam and Eve.
6. Why did Satan want to kill Jesus?
7. What is Satan trying to do with unbelievers? With Christians?
8. Who are Satan's helpers?
9. How can we overcome Satan and his helpers?
10. (a) Where will Satan be during the thousand years of our Lord's rule upon this earth?
    (b) What will Satan do at the end of the thousand years and what will be done to him then?

COURSE FOUR

LESSON I

BELIEVERS AND UNBELIEVERS
The Contrast in Relation to Sin

Try to make clear the distinction between believers and unbelievers.
The world recognizes different social "classes," but for God there are only
two classes in the world; believers and unbelievers.

1. The contrast in respect to sin.
    (a) The believer is saved.
    (b) The unbeliever is lost.
    (c) The believer is dead to sin.
    (d) The unbeliever is dead in sin.

IN YOUR school there are many grades, and in each grade there are
many different classes of pupils. Perhaps some are bright, and some
are rather stupid; some are pretty and some are homely, some are
strong and well, and some are often sick. But when God looks down at
your school, or at any other group of people in the world, He does not pay
any attention to these classes, but divides all the people into just two
groups, those who are believers and those who are unbelievers. If we could
build a long, long fence, and gather all the people in the world together,
we could put all of them either on one side of the fence or the other. No
one could be sitting on the fence, for there is no such thing as being half-
believer. It is very important to know on which side of the fence you are,
for believers have many wonderful things, and unbelievers have many
terrible things.

You know what happens the moment you believe in the Lord Jesus
Christ as your own Saviour. You are saved, for we read in Acts 16:31,
"Believe on the Lord Jesus Christ and thou shalt be saved." Many other
wonderful things happen at the same time, and we shall study some of them.

But first of all think of the difference between those who are on the
"Saved" side of the fence, and those who are on the other side—the side
of the Unbelievers. If we write "Saved" over the believers, what word shall
we write over the unbelievers? That is right, the word is "lost." Do you
know what it means to be lost? When you say you have lost your pencil,
you mean that it is gone; it is no more use to you, for you cannot find it.
When a soul is lost it is no use to God. But you may also say that a ship is

lost at sea. What do you mean by that? You may have all the pieces of the ship together in one place, but if it is a "lost ship" it is of no more use; it is damaged and destroyed. So a lost soul is damaged. God knows where it is, but it is far from Him, and in a terribly dangerous state. For if a soul stays lost until death, it will be lost forever. The good news that we have to tell to unbelievers, those who are lost, is that they can come over to the saved side of the fence right away, if they only will. The Lord Jesus is the door. By Him, if any one enters in, he will be saved. (Look up the references and discuss them, having the children mark them in their Bibles. Eph. 2:8, 9; 2 Tim. 1:9; John 3:18; 2 Cor. 4:3, 4.)

Did you know that a great many of the people whom you meet on the street are dead? They may be walking along just as you are, but if they have not believed on the Lord Jesus they are dead *in* sin (Eph. 2:1). Their souls are dead. You remember the story of the first sin. (The teacher may outline it briefly, or get it from the pupils by questioning.) God told the man and the woman that in the day they disobeyed Him, they would surely die. They did die—first their souls, then their bodies. Ever since that time, men and women have been dead as long as they were unbelievers. It is only when they believe in the Lord Jesus Christ that they receive life? What does John 3:16 say about this? And what about 1 John 5:12? The semicolon in the middle of that verse is like a fence between the saved and the lost, between those who are dead, and those who are alive.

But, strange as it may seem, Christians can be dead, too! But it is a good kind of deadness—for the Bible says that we are dead *unto* sin. We have the new eternal life which God gave us the moment we believed, and our old sinful life, God says has been crucified with Christ. So now, when Satan comes to tempt us, we can say, "I am dead to sin; I do not have to yield to your temptation." Rom. 6:11 is God's Word to us about this wonderful kind of deadness.

NOTEBOOK SUGGESTIONS: Have the children make two columns in their notebook, with a line vertically on the page to divide them. One column is to be headed "Believers;" the other, "Unbelievers." Under "Believers" they may print, in conspicuous letters, SAVED, and under "Unbelievers," LOST; then, DEAD UNTO SIN, and DEAD IN SIN. It will be well to include a Scripture reference under each. Perhaps the children would prefer to make some illustration of their own idea. In either case be sure the work looks well and the lettering done in a way to beautify their notebook.

LESSON II

BELIEVERS AND UNBELIEVERS
The Contrast in Relation to Family

Try to prevent any misapprehension as to the Fatherhood of God and the brotherhood of man.

The right to be a child.

The contrast in respect to family:

1. The unbeliever is a child of Satan.
2. The believer is a child of God by the new birth.

SUPPOSING Mary Brown should go to Ruth Jones' father, and say to him, "Daddy, will you please give me some money for church?" What do you think Mr. Jones would say? Perhaps he would think that Mary was still half asleep! Anyway, he would know that she had made a mistake in calling him Daddy. Not everyone can speak to your father as Daddy. He is your father, and the father of your brothers and sisters, but he is not the father of all your friends, too!

Some people make the bad mistake of saying that anyone in the world can speak to God as Father. They say that since He made us all, we are all His children, and we can call Him *Father*. But this is not true, and the Lord Jesus Himself is the One Who said so.

One day He was talking with the wise men and the religious men of the city of Jerusalem. Though they were wise, and though they were religious, their hearts were bad, for they hated the Lord Jesus, and wanted to kill Him. They said to Him, "We have one Father, even God." But Jesus answered, "If God were your Father, ye would love Me: for I proceeded forth and came from God . . ." (John 8:42). When the Lord Jesus said, "*If* God *were* your Father . . ." He showed very clearly that God was not their Father, for they did not love the Lord Jesus, but hated Him. But, to make it even more clear, He told them who their father was. It is a terrible thing, and if anyone but the Lord Jesus had said it, we should be much astonished, but since He said it, we know it must be true. He said, "Ye are of your father, *the Devil*" (John 8:44). So these wise religious men did not have God for their Father, but rather, Satan.

The same thing is true of all those who do not believe in the Lord Jesus Christ. They are not in the family of God; they are in the family of Satan. He is their father. Even when they pray "Our Father, which art in Heaven," and think they are praying to God, their prayers are going straight to Satan instead.

Yet no one has to be a child of Satan any longer than he wishes to be. God has made a way so that we can change families. Like all our other blessings, it is because the Lord Jesus Christ died on the cross, that we can leave the family of Satan, and come into the family of God. The Holy Spirit, speaking through John said, "But as many as received Him (the Lord Jesus) to them gave He the right to become the sons of God, even to them that believe on His name (John 1:11, 12). It is very easy, you see, to leave the terrible household of the Devil, and come into God's family. It all happens when we receive the Lord Jesus Christ, or believe on His name. Then we have the right to call God our Father, and He will call us sons and daughters.

How did you become a son or a daughter of your father and mother? You were born into their family, weren't you? It is in just the same way that you become a child of God. You are born into His family. The Lord Jesus said to Nicodemus, "Ye must be born again." When we are born again we receive a new life, the life of God, and this new birth makes us members of God's family.

NOTEBOOK SUGGESTION: Explain how climbing higher in Satan's family does not change the family. Draw the cross first.

LESSON III

BELIEVERS AND UNBELIEVERS
The Contrast as to Standing Before God

UNBELIEVERS cannot pray to God as their Father—in tact, they cannot pray to Him at all. Christ said, "No man cometh unto the Father but by Me" (John 14:6). But believers can come to Him without any fear. He is not far off, some great majestic king, of whom you need to be afraid. He is your Father. Little boys and girls in the streets of London may be afraid to speak to the king, but you may be sure that the two little princesses have no such fear. So, though God is very great, He is our Father, and we can speak with Him just as freely as we would with our earthly father.

Because we have God as our Father we want to please Him. Do you remember how you felt when you did something wrong and your father or mother knew about it? There came a barrier between you and them. It was your wrong. It is something like that, only much worse, with those who do not believe in Christ; their sin is between them and God. Nothing they can do can please Him until they receive Christ and turn from their sin. They can never be truly happy until they are Christians, though they may be gay. As soon as they really think about life and death they are like the troubled sea when it cannot rest. They may even deny that they are unhappy, but God says they are, and you must choose between believing them and believing God, Who says they have no peace (Isa. 57:20, 21).

The unbeliever is separated from God (Eph. 2:12; Isa. 59:2). When he dies he still remains separated from God (John 8:21, 24). This is what Hell really is, separation from God. Men may argue about the details of Hell, but, to say the least, it is a place far from God. When the Lord Jesus Christ died on the Cross, He took our sins, and so He was separated from God, the Father, just as we would be if we still had our sins upon us. That is why He cried out, "My God, My God, Why hast Thou forsaken Me?" (Matt. 27:46). The Lord Jesus on the cross was bearing the same thing as Hell for us. It is only because He did this that we can now be saved. It would be possible to say that the heart of Christianity is in these three sentences: I deserved Hell; Jesus Christ took my Hell; There is nothing left for me but His Heaven.

We, believers, are very near to God.   There is an old hymn:

Near, so near am I to God,	Dear, so dear am I to God,
Nearer I cannot be;	Dearer I cannot be;
For, in the person of His Son,	The love with which He loved His Son
I'm just as near as He.	Such is His love to me.

Another contrast between the believer and the unbeliever is that the unbeliever is under God's wrath, while we are under God's favor.   It is not pleasant to have someone angry with you, yet the Bible says in many places that God is angry with unbelievers (Prov. 1:24-29; John 3:18, 36; Rom. 1: 18).   No wonder He is angry with them, even though they are good, and kind and charitable, as the world uses these words.   When they refuse to accept the Lord Jesus Christ as their Saviour they are not believing God's Word about His Son, and God says that that is calling Him a liar (1 John 5: 10).   You do not have to commit some terrible crime, like murder or robbery, to be under God's wrath.   The sin of unbelief is a terrible crime to Him, even though it may seem to be small to men.   But as soon as we believe, we are taken from under God's wrath and put into His favor.

NOTEBOOK SUGGESTIONS: Review the lesson with the children as they draw.

Heaven

Unbelievers
Far from God
under wrath

THE ONLY DOOR

Believers
Near to God
under favor

But your iniquities
have separated
between you and
your God.
          Isaiah 59:2

Hell

But now in Christ
Jesus ye who sometimes
were far off made nigh
by the blood of Christ.
          Eph. 2:13

LESSON IV

BELIEVERS AND UNBELIEVERS

Try to lead the children to Christ as Saviour and Lord.

1. The unbeliever is sure of hell.
2. The believer is sure of Heaven.
3. The unbeliever waits for death and judgment.
4. The believer waits for Christ and glory.

WHEN you leave school in the afternoon you usually start for home, don't you? And when supper time comes, or bed time, you do not make a mistake and go to the house of some neighbor, thinking that it is yours! Just so believers and unbelievers have homes, and when life here is finished they will go to their own homes. But those homes are very different. One of them really isn't a home at all, for home is a lovely and loving place, and this place is everything that is not lovely and loving. But it is the place where some people must go, for it is where they belong.

Unbelievers are going down the road that leads to Hell. If they keep on by the way they are going they will get there, sooner or later. That is perfectly sure, for God's Word says so (Rev. 21:8; Psa. 9:17). The way that they are going is the way of unbelief, and there is but one end to that road. Unbelievers are just as sure of Hell as can be, though they may not realize it, or may try to disbelieve it.

Believers, on the other hand, are sure of Heaven. That is the home, and is the place where they belong. This is not because they are so much better than unbelievers (Tit. 3:5), but simply because they have believed in the Lord Jesus Christ, and God says that those who believe are saved, and are going to Heaven (1 Pet. 1:4; 2 Tim. 4:18). The Lord Jesus said He wished to have them with them forever (John 17:24), and He will be in Heaven, so believers will be with Him. We are much more sure that we shall go to Heaven than we are that we shall go home after school. Something might happen to us so that we would never get home, but if we are believers, nothing can keep us from going to Heaven.

Unbelievers have a terrible judgment yet ahead of them, when the books shall be opened, and they shall be judged according to their works. Then they shall see that even their good works could not save them, and all whose names are not written in the book of life will be cast into Hell

(Rev. 20:12, 13). Unsaved men have nothing to look forward to but death, and then judgment (Heb. 9:27).

But saved people, those who believe, do not have to look forward to anything like that. They may die, yes, but their death will be just a moment between earth and Heaven. Paul even wanted to die, so he could go to be with Christ (Phil. 1:21, 23). But believers may not die, for Christ may come at any moment, and then they would go to Heaven without dying (1 Cor. 15:51, 52; Phil. 3:20, 21; Heb. 9:28). And for believers there is waiting no judgment for sin, for Christ bore all that on the cross (John 5:24). Only glory waits for them, not because they deserve it, but because God has graciously chosen to give it to all who believe (Rom. 8:18).

Many Chinese buy their coffins years before they are going to die, and keep them in their homes, so that they will be ready when needed. A wealthy Chinese, who had a most beautiful coffin, became a Christian. He soon had some Chinese characters painted on each end of his coffin, saying that when the time came for his funeral, he wanted the people of the town to see where he was going. On the front end of the coffin he had the words for "The dead in Christ shall rise" (1 Thess. 4:16). On the back end there were the words, "Even so, come, Lord Jesus" (Rev. 22:20). What a change in his thinking, for before he had become a believer all he had thought about was that he would be dead for ever.

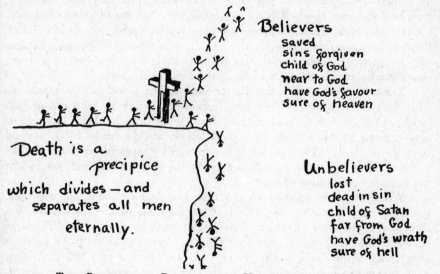

Believers
saved
sins forgiven
child of God
near to God
have God's favour
sure of heaven

Death is a precipice
which divides — and
separates all men
eternally.

Unbelievers
lost
dead in sin
child of Satan
far from God
have God's wrath
sure of hell

TEST QUESTIONS ON BELIEVERS AND UNBELIEVERS ON PAGE 188.

LESSON V

FULL ASSURANCE

Full Assurance is Based Upon Christ's Work

I ONCE heard a man say, "I am just as sure that I am going to be in Heaven as I am sure Christ is going to be there." I thought the man must be either very good, or very proud. But then, as I came to know the Bible I learned that he had no goodness in himself and that he was not a proud man. He knew God and He knew the Bible, therefore, he could not say anything else than that he was as sure he would be in Heaven as he was sure Christ would be there.

What does God demand of us in order that we reach Heaven? He cannot demand anything less than perfection, for He, Himself, is perfect, and if He would let imperfect people into His Heaven, He would not have a perfect standard. You have seen an old-fashioned platform scales. If you put a pound weight in one side you must put how much in the other side to make it balance. One pound. Ten ounces will not do it. And if the scales are properly adjusted you will have to put sixteen ounces, for not even fifteen and a fraction ounces will change the balance.

There are three kinds of people in the world: the very bad, the ordinary and the very good. Let us weigh the very bad man in God's balance. He is a murderer, thief, liar and anything else you wish to call him. But there is honour among thieves, the world's proverb says. So we will give him two ounces of good works for his account. But two ounces will not swing the balance and we find him in the heap of the lost.

Then we come to a much better man as the world counts goodness. This man is the ordinary citizen. He is good enough to keep out of jail, but he is bad enough to do everything that he wants to do. He is an amiable sinner, liked by his friends as a good fellow, always ready to do a good turn for anybody. He has, we will say, eight ounces of goodness for his account. But eight ounces will not swing the balance and we find him in the same heap as those who are lost.

When we have weighed all the very bad and all the average people, there are very few who are left. But we take one of these few, and find that he is a professor of ethics. That means that he studies the differences between right and wrong. He does the very best he can do to be right in everything he does and thinks. Everybody says he is a very fine man, that he would make a wonderful judge, that he is the finest man they know.

Mother says that she wishes her Johnny would grow up to be like him, he is such a fine man. So we ask him how many ounces he has. Is he perfect? Oh no! He readily admits that he is not perfect. He knows he is better than the bandit and he says he tries to do the best he can do in all things. If we are going to give one man two ounces and another eight, he says we might count him nine or ten. But we know that he is very modest, so we put thirteen ounces to his account. But thirteen ounces will not swing the balance and we find this very good professor in the same heap as the bandits and the average people. Sometimes this makes such people angry. They want to know what kind of God we have Who counts them the same as the worst men on earth. But our God is a God of holiness, who demands perfection. But who, then, can be saved? *All,* the bad, the ordinary and the very good, *all* are found to be sinners. But just here God shows us the cross of Jesus Christ. He tells us that He has provided His own righteousness as a gift, and that He will put it to our account if we will come to Him with our hands emptied of all our two, eight or thirteen ounces of our own good works. So we come with nothing of our own and, by faith, we receive the gift of the righteousness of God in Christ. We go with that to the balances of God and put Christ over against God's demand for perfection. The scale balances, and God takes us into His Heaven, not on our own incomplete goodness, but on the basis of the perfection of Christ. By faith we lay hold on Christ and offer Him back to God. God then takes us into Heaven because of what Christ is. So we can have full assurance because God has found in Christ all that He must demand of us, and we are for ever free.

NOTEBOOK SUGGESTIONS: Have the children choose a verse to write beneath the picture.

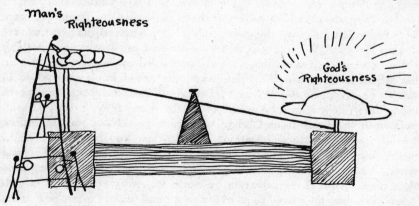

LESSON VI

FULL ASSURANCE

Try to lead the children to full assurance of their position in Christ.

1. What full assurance is.
2. The completeness of the atonement.

IF I should ask you, "Are you alive?" you would not answer, "I guess so," would you? You would know surely that you were living. There are some things that it is foolish to be in doubt about. It is one of these things that we are going to talk about today, and yet there are many people who are not sure about it. Perhaps you are not sure yourself, but when we finish the lesson, you will be.

If I should ask you, "Are you saved?" what would be your answer? Many people would say, "I hope so," or "I am trying to be," or "I hope someday I shall be." But those are all very foolish answers. You and I are going to find out why. For no one who knows the Bible could give an uncertain answer. Every Christian should have full assurance. Full assurance is *the certainty that you are saved.* Are you certain that you are saved, or are you a "guess so" Christian? We will look at what God's Word says, to find out why and how we are certain of our salvation.

The first thing we need to know is how we are saved. Can you tell me and give me a verse for it? (The class should give you Acts 16:31, and say that they are saved by believing that Christ died for them. If there is any hesitation, clear up this point fully.) Are we saved by good works? Look up Eph. 2:8, 9. In these verses we see that our works have nothing at all to do with our salvation. We are not saved by what we do, but by what Christ did. When the Philippian jailer asked Paul what to do in order to be saved, he did not say, "Believe in the Lord Jesus, and go to church," or, "Believe and be good," or "Believe and pray." He just said, "Believe in the Lord Jesus Christ." There is no AND about salvation. Now let me ask you three questions. 1. How can you be saved? (Right answer, Acts 16:31.) 2. Do you believe in the Lord Jesus Christ? (Usual answer, Yes.) 3. Are you saved? (Probably they will answer Yes, unless they have had the salvation by works idea very strongly ingrained. If they have, you may have to go over this ground several times.) You see

the only answer you could give is Yes, for God says if you believe you *are
saved*. If you say you are not, you are making out that God does not tell
the truth.

The reason why we are saved only by believing that Christ died for us
on the cross, is that when He died, he FINISHED the work of salvation.
Do you remember the story of that dark hour when Christ died? Do you
remember those words that He said then? They were very important.
We will read them in John 19:30. "It is finished," were His words. He
meant that the great work of salvation was all done. In John 17:4 we find
the same words. Now look up Heb. 1:3. There we find that He purged
(or washed away) our sins by *Himself*. He did not need any help. He did
it by dying on the cross for us.

It is because of this that we are so sure we are saved. We believe that
He did die for us, and it is by His dying, and nothing else that we are saved.
So we have full assurance that we are saved, because Christ finished the
work of salvation on the cross.

NOTEBOOK SUGGESTIONS: Be sure the children can recite Psalm 71:3 when they have
finished their illustration.

LESSON VII

FULL ASSURANCE

Full Assurance is Based on the Work and Word of Christ

IF YOU knew someone who simply couldn't tell a lie, you would always believe that person's word, wouldn't you? You do know Someone like that—but there is only One like that in the universe. God cannot lie. He cannot even make a mistake (Read Titus 1:2).

Whether or not you have full assurance depends exactly upon what you think about God. Suppose that a boy wanted money to go on a vacation. He knew that his father and mother could not afford to send him, but he still wanted to go. He had an uncle who came to dinner one evening, saw the boy disappointed and asked him what was the matter. The boy told his uncle, who patted him on the back and said, "Come down to my office on Saturday morning, and I will give you a check for the full amount. I will be delighted to let you have that vacation as a gift from me."

What do you think the boy would do? He telephones his chum a few minutes later. How is he going to speak to his chum? It all depends on what he thinks of his uncle and his uncle's word. One of two conversations may take place. He may take the phone and say, "Oh, Bill, what do you think? My uncle is giving me the vacation trip. It is all settled. I am to go to his office on Saturday and get the money. Isn't that wonderful?

Or else he might say to his friend, "Oh, I would like to go well enough, but there is no hope. My old bragging uncle was here at dinner and told me that he would give me a check for the full amount if I came to his office on Saturday, but if I went his clerk would tell me that the old fellow had to go to Timbuktu or somewhere else on a sudden trip, and that there was no check.

Now we have a Heavenly Father Who cannot lie. His very name is truth. Christ said, "I am the truth" (John 14:6). That is why David is able to sing of Him, "According to Thy Name, O God, so is Thy praise unto the ends of the earth" (Ps. 48:10). Solomon, the wisest man who ever lived, said, "The name of the Lord is a strong tower; the righteous runneth into it and is safe" (Prov. 18:10).

One of His best known promises is John 3:16. Once I was in a class where the teacher called one of us to the blackboard, gave us a text, made us write an outline for our talk, then turn around and give it to the class. A Chinese student was given John 3:16. He went to the board and apologized to the class that he did not know English very well, and that he would have to be sure of the grammar of the verse. So he said, "The subject is *God*. The verb is *loved*. The object is *world*." Then after a moment he said, "Then there is *God* a second time, with another verb, *gave*. The object of this is *Son*." He kept writing on the blackboard and it looked like this when he had finished the whole verse.

God	Loved	World
God	Gave	Son
Whosoever	Believeth	Him
Whosoever	Shall have	Life

Then he drew a line between the first two and the second two, and said, "The first two are God's part, and they are in the past tense. The second two are man's part and they are in the present tense. All God's work is finished. His gift has been given. Our part remains to be done. We must believe. But if we believe we have everlasting life." We saw that we were getting much more than a lesson in grammar. We were learning that when God promises, He puts it in the past tense, and that when we do what we are told to do, we may be sure that He keeps His Word. It all depends on Him. Ask yourself the following questions. Do I believe that God loved me? Did God give His Son to die for me? Have I believed in Him as best I know? Do I *have*, right now, what He says I have when I believe? Do I have life eternal?

NOTEBOOK SUGGESTIONS: As the children draw emphasize that we are safe in trusting the Lord.

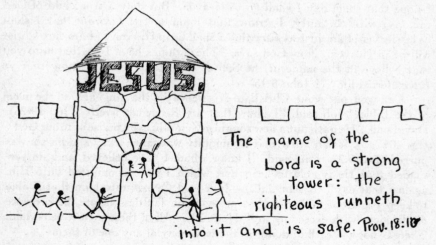

The name of the Lord is a strong tower: the righteous runneth into it and is safe. Prov. 18:10

LESSON VIII

FULL ASSURANCE

Try to lead the children to full assurance of their own salvation.
Full assurance is based on the promises of God.

OUR assurance of salvation does not depend upon what we are or what we have done, but upon what Christ is and what He has done. As soon as we understand that fact we will not be afraid to step out on the promises of God.

I am going to misquote a verse. If anybody knows what is wrong do not speak out but simply hold up your hand. If you do not know what is wrong with the verse, you are not very advanced in knowledge of what it means to be a Christian. If you know what is wrong when I misquote it, you are already making progress, and will soon stop being a babe in Christ and will begin to be grown up in Christ. Here is the misquoted verse. These things have I written unto you that believe in the name of the Son of God that ye may hope that ye will have eternal life. That is *not* the Word of God.

Before I give you the reference and quote the verse rightly let me ask you a question. Is there any difference between saying, I hope that I will some day have a million dollars, and in saying, I know that I now have a million dollars? Only a very rich man could say the latter, but any vagabond could say the first. So, anybody can say, and most people do say, I hope that some day I shall go to Heaven. But only a true child of God can say, with certainty, I *know* that I am saved; I *know* that I shall be in Heaven; I am just as *sure* that I shall be in Heaven as I am sure Christ will be in Heaven. Now God says, "These things have I written unto you that believe in the name of the Son of God, that ye may *know* that ye *have* eternal life" (1 John 5:13).

Can you put your Christian experience in the language of the men of the Bible? Job said, "I know that my Redeemer liveth" (Job 19:25). David said, "He hath put a new song in my mouth, even praise unto our God" (Ps. 40: 2, 3). Isaiah knew that his iniquity was taken away and his sin was purged (Isa. 6:7). Paul said, "I know whom I have believed, and am persuaded that He is able to keep that which I have committed unto Him against that day" (2 Tim. 1:12). Jude said, "Now unto Him that is able to keep you from falling, and to present you faultless before the presence of His glory with exceeding joy" (Jude 24). All of these men were certain. There is not a breath of doubt in the testimony of any one of them.

We have already seen what John said, and it is worth while to look at the passage in which he said it. Turn to 1 John 5 and begin with the 9th verse. "If we receive the witness of men, the witness of God is greater . . ." You do receive the witness of men. You believe the train schedules, and you go to the station ten minutes before the hour announced for the train departure instead of ten minutes afterwards, because you believe that the train·will go at the hour the company has announced. You go to church on Sunday morning and not on Tuesday morning, because the services are announced for Sunday and not for Tuesday and you believe the announcement. God says that if you believe what men say you should believe even more in what He says, for His witness is greater, and He cannot lie.

What is His witness? What has He said? "This is the witness of God which He hath testified of His Son. He that believeth on the Son of God hath the witness in Himself" (1 John 5:10). When we tell you that the Bible is true and that Jesus died for you, there is a voice in your heart which says, This is true! This is true! That is the voice of the Holy Spirit, and it is the witness that God gives to your spirit, that His Word is true, and that you may know that you have eternal life. If you do not believe God's record, the next verse says that your unbelief makes God a liar. What a terrible thing to do! Yet there are many Christians who do this all the time by trying to teach that we may not know for certain that we have eternal life as a present possession. When God says that we may know that we have, do not let the devil cheat you out of your possessions by making you think you have to sit around and merely hope so.

NOTEBOOK SUGGESTION: Let the children choose a verse t o write beneath the picture

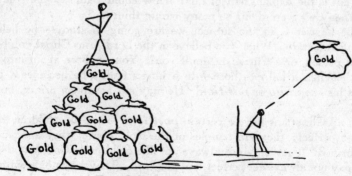

TEST QUESTIONS ON PAGE 188.

LESSON IX

STANDING AND STATE OR POSITION AND CONDITION

1. Definition of terms.
2. Illustrations of Corinth and the Philippian jailer.

IN PAUL'S letter to the Church at Corinth, he says some things that seem to be contradictions. In one place he tells them they are very good and in other places speaks to them sternly about some terrible sins they had committed. Let us read together 1 Cor. 1:4-8. Those words sound like a picture of some Christians who are just about perfect, don't they? But look at verse 11. There Paul says he has heard that there are "contentions"—and that means fights—among them. Christians who are doing God's will do not fight among themselves. Then look at chapter 3:3. Again we find that there are divisions among them and that they "walk as men," which means that they act like unsaved men. That does not sound like perfect Christians either. But this is not the worst, for in 5:1 we find that there was a terrible sin among them, a sin that was so bad that even unbelievers did not talk about it. And in the next verse it says that they were not even sorry, but seemed to be proud in the midst of it all. Then chapter six shows that they were having law suits between themselves. This is another thing that is very wrong for Christians. And in chapter eleven we find that some of them even were drunk at the communion table.

What is the explanation of this? How could Paul say that they were good when they were doing so many wrong things?

The answer is in the subject we are going to study—the believer's standing and state. When you believe in the Lord Jesus Christ you become a saved person, or a Christian, don't you? You are born again into God's family. When a baby is born into a king's family he becomes a prince. That is his *standing* or *position*. He may not act like a prince, but he is one.

So all Christians have a certain *position*. They are children of God; they are perfect; they are temples of the Holy Spirit; they are sanctified and glorified. They may not always act like children of God, but they are. They may not always act perfect, but they are. They may not seem to have the Holy Spirit but they have. They have all these things because they have been born again. Their *standing* is the way God looks at them. The way they act is called their *state* or *condition*. Their state ought to be just like their standing, but sometimes it takes many years for them to learn to act like what they are. In Acts 16:22-34, we have the story of a brutal jailer who was saved. (Tell the story.) No doubt he had a hard evil face, for he was a heathen. He was cruel to Paul and Silas. And yet he did come to believe in the Lord Jesus, and was saved. The moment he believed, he was born again. At once he was a child of God, though his face was just about the same. It would take some time before he would begin to look like a child of God. As soon as he believed, God counted him as perfect, yet he would not act perfect till he got to Heaven. His *standing* was what God made him the moment he believed. His *state* was the way he lived. Our standing comes from the fact that we have the new nature, which is eternal life, the life of Christ. Our State comes from the fact that our old nature can never be anything other than the filthy thing God declares it to be. We must yield it to the Lord for daily death with Christ.

NOTEBOOK SUGGESTION: Have the children select a verse to write beneath the illustration.

Our
State
is the way
we live on
Earth.

In
christ
Our
Standing
is the way
God sees us
in
christ.

LESSON X

STANDING AND STATE

Try to lead the children to realize their standing in Christ so that they
may be drawn to surrender themselves to the Lord afresh.

Two or three times during the course of the lesson stop and have the
pupils define "position," "condition," "standing" and "state" for you,
so that you are sure that they know what they are talking about. Reread
"Teaching Hints."

1. How we receive our standing:
2. Our standing as:
    (a) Sons.
    (b) Heirs.
    (c) Justified.

HOW can a baby become a prince? There is only one way. He must
be born into the family of a king. Only the son of a king is a prince.
Just so there is only one way in which we can receive the standing
of children of God. We must be born into His family—that is, born again.
You know how one can be born again, do you not? (Go over that subject
clearly.) When we are born again into God's family the standing or position
that we receive is far more wonderful than that of a prince in this world.

First of all, when we are born again we receive the position of children
of God. John 1:12 tells us that God gives to as many as believe on His name
the right to be called the sons of God. It does not say that we always act
like children of God. But that is our position. God says we are His children.
Yet in 2 Cor. 6:17, 18 He tells us to come out from among unbelievers and
not to be with them or act like them, and He will be our Father and we will
be His sons and daughters. How can that be, if we are already His children?
This verse is not talking about our position, but about our condition. If
we do what this verse says, we shall live like God's sons and daughters, and
He will be able to act as a Father to us, more than ever before.

Because we are the children of God, we have many wonderful privileges.
We have His love and care, and we are made His heirs. A person's heir is
his son, or some other person who receives that other person's possessions
when he dies. God says we are His heirs, which means that He is giving us
all He has, though of course He can never die. Look up 1 Pet. 1:4; Rom.
8:16, 17. Think of all the things which God possesses! The whole earth is
His, and the sun, moon and stars. We may not even own a little piece of the

earth, but really it is all ours, because we are heirs of God. Our condition
may be one of poverty, but in our position we are rich—heirs of a King!

More important to us than what God has, is that which God *is*. We
are heirs of His holiness, His love, His gentleness, His peace, His goodness and all the other attributes which are revealed to us in Christ. We
are to be like Him when He comes (1 John 3:2), but we are to grow more
like Him now day by day as our condition is changed little by little to be
more like our position.

In the last lesson, in the picture, we saw that our standing or position
is what we are *in* Christ. Read any place in Paul's epistles and see if you
can find one of the more than one hundred verses where the believer is said
to be *in* Christ. It would be a good thing for you to draw a circle around
the word *in* every time you find it in front of a name of Christ or a pro-
noun representing Him in all of the epistles. In Ephesians the first chapter
you will find this little word nine times. We were placed *in* Christ the
moment we were saved.

NOTEBOOK SUGGESTION: Let the children choose a verse to write beneath the picture.

LESSON XI

STANDING AND STATE

Do not fail to take account of the test which goes with these lessons. The questions cover the important points, and you should be sure that each child has them in mind clearly even before the test is given.

Our standing as:
(d) Kings and priests.
(e) Perfect.
(f) Temples of the Holy Spirit.
(g) Glorified.

THE story is told of a nobleman's second son who, through sin, had to leave England for Canada. Each quarter he received a certain sum of money which was quickly spent and he then resorted to various means of earning his living. One day while he was working in a shop for about fifteen dollars a week, he was visited by a lawyer who told him that his father had died and that his older brother had been killed in a motor accident. He was now heir to the title. His standing was noble, he was eligible to take his seat in the House of Lords. His state was that of a working man, earning a low wage and living a miserable existence. Our standing is in Christ and we must learn to live according to it. We are sons of God, heirs, justified! And that is only part of it.

We are also Kings and Priests. Did you know you were a king? Perhaps you do not have a crown, but God says you are a king, and some day you shall reign. You will sit with Him on His throne. We are also priests. The priests, in Old Testament times, were those who came into the temple, the place where God dwelt. Since Christ died, and because we believe in Him, we are allowed to be in His presence all the time. You remember that when Christ died, the veil in the temple was torn in two from the top to the bottom. Then the holy of holies, where God dwelt, was open so that all could see. This meant that we need no longer stay outside, but could come right into God's presence. So now we are priests. We can come boldly right to God's throne (Heb. 4:16; Rev. 1:5, 6; 5:10).

But even this is not all our position. God says we are perfect. We surely do not look perfect or feel perfect, but God looks at us through the Lord Jesus Christ, and says we are perfect. Our state is very imperfect, but our standing is perfect. It is the new nature that is perfect and the old nature that is imperfect. Of our standing God writes, "Whosoever is born of God doth not commit sin; for His seed remaineth in him: and he cannot sin, because he is born of God" (1 John 3:9). Of our state, God writes, "For I know that in me, that is in my flesh, dwelleth no good thing" (Rom. 7:18).

Then too we are the dwelling places of the Holy Spirit. God lives in you, if you are a Christian. 1 Cor. 6:19. He is within us and will never leave us. In Old Testament times God lived in the temple. Now His temple is our hearts. Too often we forget this, and act as though we belonged to ourselves, but our standing remains the same. He is within us forever.

Another wonderful part of our standing is that we are glorified. Rom. 8:30 says "whom He did predestinate, them He also called; and whom He called, them He also justified (you remember what that means); and whom He justified, them He also glorified." All this is in the past tense, which means that it is done already. But are you glorified? Do you look and act like Jesus? That is what it means to be glorified. No you will not be glorified till Jesus comes, and yet you are glorified already. That is just the difference between state and standing.

We are, by our standing, Sons of God (John 1:12); heirs (1 Pet. 1:4); justified (Rom. 5:1); kings and priests (Rev. 1:5, 6; 5:10); perfect (Heb. 10:14); temples of the Spirit (1 Cor. 6:19); glorified (Rom. 8:30).

NOTEBOOK SUGGESTION: Let the pupils make a list of the things that compose our standing.

A King .... and kingly

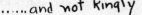

......and not kingly

LESSON XII

STANDING AND STATE

Don't let the fact of our imperfect condition form an excuse for your
pupils for living on a low level. This lesson should remedy any thought in
that direction.

1. The Spirit's desire to make us perfect.
2. His method of working.

IT IS true that our condition is not equal to our position, but God wants
to make it so. That is His purpose. He is going to make us just like
the Lord Jesus Christ (Rom. 8:29; 1 John 3:2). He is not satisfied
with our living imperfect lives, but wants us to become more and more
perfect in our state day by day. When He finishes His work in us, our
state and our standing will be both just alike.

When your mother starts to embroider a fine piece of linen, she buys
a stencil and presses the design on the linen with a hot iron. The whole
plan of the work is there; she then proceeds to spend days, and sometimes
months, embroidering each little bit according to the plan. So, from the
very first moment we are saved, God puts Christ upon us; this is our position. He then proceeds to work within us that we may be conformed to
that image so that our condition may be nearer to what we are in God's
sight, in Christ.

How will God accomplish His purpose? How can He make us like the
Lord Jesus? One way is by the Bible. The Bible can make us like the
Lord Jesus. In 2 Cor. 3:18 we read that we behold as in a glass (or mirror,
which means the Bible) the glory of the Lord, and are changed into the
same image by the Spirit of the Lord. When you look into the Bible you
find the Lord Jesus there. It tells about Him, and all the wonderful things
He does. The Holy Spirit takes the words of that wonderful Book, and
somehow, uses them to make us more like the Lord Jesus. The more you read
your Bible, and learn verses from it, the more quickly the Holy Spirit can
make your state like your standing. The Lord Jesus prayed the Father,
asking Him to do this. He said, "Sanctify them through Thy truth; Thy
Word is truth" (John 17:17). This could well be translated: Make them

holy through Bible study. That is why we are so interested in having you know all that you can about this wonderful book.

You must be willing to do what God wants you to. He is very patient, and He will not make you do what is right, unless you want to. But if you are willing to do the things that please Him, it will be much easier for Him to make you like the Lord Jesus. Paul wrote to the Romans, beseeching them to yield to the Lord (Rom. 12:1).

Prayer will help too. The more you talk with the Lord, the better you will come to know Him, and it is when you know Him that you will become more like Him. You know that you learn to recognize the voices of people that live in your home, and you even learn to recognize their step on the stairs. We should learn to live so closely to God, and to spend time with Him so that we can know His voice when He speaks to us, and learn to obey.

Of course we shall never in this world be perfect in our state, for we have the old nature within us, and that is always bad. But when the Lord Jesus comes the work will be finished, and we shall be made just exactly like Him.

NOTEBOOK SUGGESTION: Dictate the following:

> The accompanying diagram illustrates the standing and state of the believer—his standing perfect, indicated by the horizontal line; his state, becoming more and more like his standing as he grows in grace, indicated by the broken line, until finally, at the coming of the Lord, the work is completed.
> Have the children select two verses to write under this diagram. Encourage them to write as neatly and as artistically as they can.

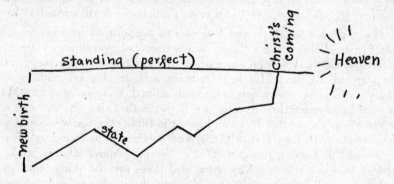

TEST QUESTIONS ON STANDING AND STATE ON PAGE 189.

LESSON XIII

MAN

There is a paragraph in the hints for teachers that refers especially to this
section. It should be read.

WE CANNOT imagine a time when there was nothing, nothing,
nothing anywhere—no sun, no stars, no world. But there was
such a time, and then, suddenly, God spoke, and all things were
created (Gen. 1:1). The sun flashed forth, the stars and moon shone out at
night, and the world turned steadily on its axis. Man was not created at
that moment, but later, perhaps thousands or even millions of years later.
The Bible does not say how long it was before the very first creation of
Gen. 1:1 and the creation of animals, fishes, plants, and finally man.

Man was different from anything else that God had created, for man
had understanding. God the Father, Son and Spirit spoke together about
the creation of man, saying, "Let Us make man in Our image, after Our
likeness." It is wonderful to think that man was made something like
God (Gen. 1:26, 27). The way in which God made man is described in
Gen. 2:7. God formed the body of man from the dust of the earth. Some-
what as you use modeling clay, perhaps, only so much more wonderfully,
God formed each part of man. Then He breathed into man's nostrils the
breath of life, His own breath, and man became alive, a living soul. We
cannot understand all this, but God tells us this is how it was done, and so
we believe it. When we get to Heaven, perhaps God will explain it to us.

Many people today do not believe this account of creation from the
Bible. Instead they have a theory which they call evolution. They teach
that on the earth (and who knows how the earth got here?) there was a
little tiny cell of life. This kept growing and developing, century after
century, until it became a fish, a bird, an animal, and finally man. Many
wise men have spent their lives trying to prove that this was the way man
came to be on the earth. But you know the Bible says the wisdom of men
is foolishness with God (1 Cor. 1:20) and so these wise sounding theories
are foolish if they contradict God's Word. Many things make it
seem as though evolution were true, and these are the things that those
who believe it will teach you. They do not tell you about the many things
that make it seem impossible, though there are such. Anyway, God cannot

be mistaken, and He tells us in Genesis just how it was done.   If man had been made first as some kind of animal, he would not be in the image of God, would he?   No, the first man was perfect, with a wonderful mind, and a pure heart.   God made him so when He created him.   It is interesting to know that no man in the world who is truly born again, in the sense that he believes himself to be a lost sinner, saved only by the death of Jesus Christ, eternal Son of God, believes that man came up from the animals. A very great scientist, who is a fine Christian, when asked by another scientist why he did not believe in evolution, answered that when the problem of the new birth was answered, then men could begin to study these other questions without making mistakes.

God created man for His own glory, and also so that He might have him for a friend.   He made him perfectly good and wise so that He could enjoy being with him.   Gen. 3:8 tells how God came to speak to man at evening time when it was cool and beautiful in the Garden of Eden.   If man had only remained good instead of sinning, he would have been a glory to God, for good things always please and glorify Him.   But next week we are to see the terrible thing that happened in that Garden home that had been so happy, both for the man and woman and for God.

NOTEBOOK SUGGESTION: Bring cardboard discs for the children to draw around.

So God created MAN
in His own image Gen1 27
and for His glory. Col 1:16

God has made foolish the wisdom of this world   ICor 1:20

LESSON XIV

MAN

Try to lead the children to Christ as Saviour and Lord.

Do not by any means try to smooth over the fact of the fall and the resulting sin and misery. The children's hope is not in being kind to these things, but in seeing them early enough to avoid them by taking Christ as their Saviour. There is no fear of painting too dark a picture of man's sinfulness.

1. The cause ot the fall.
2. The manner of the fall.
3. The immediate effects of the fall.

IT WOULD have been very wonderful if the man and woman could have lived happily forever in the garden of Eden, but that was far from the case. We do not know how long they were happy and pure of heart, for the Bible does not say. But it does tell us the story of their fall.

God had given the man and woman just one command. He did not tell them not to steal, for everything in the world was theirs! He did not tell them not to covet their neighbors' things, for they had no neighbors. But He did tell them that they were not to eat the fruit that grew on a tree in the middle of the Garden, a tree called the tree of the knowledge of good and evil. There were many, many other fruit trees of all kinds in the Garden, so that they could not possibly be hungry.

Satan heard the command God gave them, and he hated God and and wanted to steal everything he could from Him. So he went about seeking to make the man and woman disobey. He was very clever about it. The story is told in Gen. 3. (The teacher may wish to have the story read in class, each pupil reading a verse in succession; discussing the whole afterwards). He took the form of a beautiful animal, the serpent—they were not ugly as they are today—and came and spoke to the woman. Possibly the woman had seen so many wonderful things since God had made her that it did not surprise her when the serpent spoke to her. He said, "Has God said you should not eat of the tree?" She answered that he had. Then Satan went on, full of his lies, saying that the fruit would really be good for them, and would make them like God. He hinted that God was very cruel to tell them not to eat the fruit. The woman was deceived by his fair speeches. and took the fruit and ate it. This was disobedience—

sin, the first sin that had ever come into this new beautiful earth. It was soon followed by another, for Adam ate some of the fruit too. But Adam's sin was worse than the woman's, for she thought she was doing a good thing and making herself and her husband like God. She was deceived (1 Tim. 2:14). But when she brought the fruit to Adam, he knew that it was wrong, knew that he was disobeying, and deliberately took the fruit and ate it, thus making himself a rebel against God.

Perhaps eating the fruit seems like a "little" sin to you, but any disobedience to God, no matter how little it seems, is real sin, and just as bad as murder or thievery. This first sin in the world has caused all the other sin, and all the pain and misery that has come since.

When God came down that evening to talk with the man and woman, they were not waiting for Him as usual. Sin had made them ashamed and they had hidden in the bushes. God called to them, and found them. Adam blamed his sin on the woman, and she blamed the serpent. God cursed the serpent, and then turned to the man and woman. He told them they would have toil and pain and sorrow, and He had to put them out of the Garden so that they would not eat another fruit that would make them live for ever just as they were. It would be terrible for men to have to live for ever and ever just as they are, in sin. But God had something far better for them. He would give them new life and they would live for ever, but like Christ. Sin is at the bottom of all trouble, and this first sin is the beginning of all trouble.

NOTEBOOK SUGGESTIONS: Draw trees first, then outline hills, etc.

Earth and man's heart:
a garden.

Earth and man's heart:
a desert.

LESSON XV

MAN

Show the children that they fell in Adam's sin, and that they can be saved
only by Christ.
Effects of the fall: Spiritual death, guilt, corruption, transgressions.

THE thorns and thistles and the pain and suffering were the least part
of the bad things which came as a result of the fall. They seemed
bad enough, but there were some things that were worse. Back in
Gen. 1:27 God had told Adam that in the day that he ate of the forbidden
fruit he would surely die. When he did eat the fruit, and yet did not fall
dead, he may have thought God had deceived him. But God had not, for
Adam was really dead, in a much worse way than if he had suddenly fallen
over and died. For his soul was dead. "The soul that sinneth, it shall
die," says the Lord (Ezek. 18:20). A dead soul is one that is separated from
God, just as a dead body is one which is separated from the soul. As soon as
Adam sinned, he was separated from God, for God is too righteous even to
look upon iniquity (Hab. 1:13).

The worst of all this was that all Adam's children, and their children,
and all men who are descended from Adam have been born with dead souls.
Just as a cat's babies are kittens, and a dog's babies are puppies and not some
other kind of animal, so the children of a man with a dead soul were people
with dead souls (1 Cor. 15:22).

As soon as Adam sinned he became guilty. We can understand that
easily. As soon as a man murders he becomes guilty of murder. As soon as
Adam sinned against God by disobedience, he became guilty of sin. And
since God is a just God, He cannot forget that guilt, or excuse it. He can
forgive it through Christ, but that is not the same as excusing it (Ex. 34:7).
But not only Adam, but all his descendents became guilty too. Adam was
the first man, the father of all other men, and the head of the race. What he
did was just the same as if everyone, even you and I, had done it. That was
the arrangement that God had made. So you and I, even when we were
babies, were guilty, because of the sin that Adam committed, and before
we were guilty for our own sins. God says we are guilty by nature, guilty
by choice, and guilty because He has announced that we are guilty. That
is why David said he was a sinner before he was born (Ps. 51:5).

There is sin in every heart in the world. Even a tiny baby has a sinful heart, for he inherits it from his parents, and they in turn from theirs, until we go all the way back to Adam. When the baby grows this sinfulness shows itself in acts which are sinful. We are so sinful that we cannot do anything to please God (Rom. 8:8). There is nothing in us that is good. Our minds are evil, for we think evil thoughts. Our hearts are evil, for they have evil feelings. Our bodies are even the channels for many wicked deeds. None of this would have been true had it not been for Adam's sin.

Not only are all men spiritually dead, guilty before God, and corrupt in every part of their nature, but everyone has sinned (Rom. 3:23). The badness in us comes out in bad deeds. All this is because of the first sin, just as all the water in the river comes from the springs at its source. We could never get rid of this terrible stream of sin by ourselves, but God has made a way to free us through the Lord Jesus Christ.

NOTEBOOK SUGGESTION: Let the children make their own corner design.

Effects of the fall on the human race

① separated from God
spiritual death
Gen 1.17 Ezek 18:20
I Cor 15 22

② Guilt
Rom 5:18

③ weight of
sin
Rom 3 23

④ corruption
selfishness
lying
dishonesty
worldliness
hatred

LESSON XVI

MAN

Try to lead the children to Christ as Saviour and Lord.

1. The promise of a redeemer.
2. The plan of redemption in foreview.
3. Imputation.

WE CANNOT study about the fall of man without studying about God's way of saving men, for He planned that even, before He created the world (Eph. 1:4). And just as soon as man sinned, God came offering the remedy for sin. (The story is to be found in Gen. 3: 8-21. Tell it, bringing out the following points.) When God spoke to the serpent, or really to the Devil who was in the body of the serpent, He spoke of a Coming One Who should be the "Seed of the woman." This referred to Jesus, for you know He was the Son of Mary, a woman, but had no earthly father. God tells us in the New Testament that when He used the word "seed" in the singular instead of "seeds" in the plural, He was talking about Christ and not about mere children (Gal. 3:16). God in Heaven was His father. God said that this one should bruise the serpent's head—and when a serpent's head is bruised he is destroyed, so that this means that He should destroy Satan. But He added that the serpent should bruise His heel. This Satan did at the cross, for it was he who caused Christ to be put to death, by giving his hatred to the wicked men who delivered Him to die. But it was Christ, made sin for us, Who becomes the Deliverer for us, and the One Who destroys Satan.

In the same chapter God gave a little picture of the way of salvation. Adam and his wife were naked, for they had sinned, and they had tried to make clothing of large leaves. But these were quite useless, and the Lord came and made them clothing of skins. In order to have skins, some animal had to be killed. Very likely God slew a lamb in order to make a covering for these sinful people. Many years later another lamb, the Lamb of God which taketh away the sin of the world, would be slain to make a covering for the whole sinful race of men. So what God did there in the Garden of Eden was a picture of what He would do for men on the cross.

But this is not all. You remember that because Adam sinned, all men since have been sinners, guilty, corrupt and full of transgressions. This was because God had made an agreement with him, not for himself only, but for all his descendants. If he had been righteous all his descendants would have been righteous. But because he sinned, we are all sinners. God made another covenant like that with the Lord Jesus, not for Himself only, but for all who would believe in Him. By that agreement, just as Adam's sin came on all, so Christ's righteousness came on all who believed in Him. It is for this reason that Christ is called "the last Adam." Read carefully the two great passages teaching this truth, Rom. 5:12-21; 1 Cor. 15:45-49. Christ never sinned; He kept God's law perfectly. So we who believe in Him, being in God's agreement or covenant, are considered as perfectly righteous by God. It is a terrible thing to be a child of "the first Adam" and so sinful and guilty. We cannot help that, for we are all descendants of Adam. But we can get out of that old relationship any time we wish by believing in Jesus. Then we are in the new agreement—saved, and accepted in the Lord Jesus Christ. Then we are no longer "in Adam" but "in Christ," and all His goodness is counted as ours. It is something like a bank account. All Adam's bad account was charged to us, but when we believed, all the Lord Jesus' good account was given over to us. So we have all the goodness we need to be acceptable to God, and allowed to live in Heaven with Him.

NOTEBOOK SUGGESTION: Adam's children have spiritual death, guilt, corruption and sinful acts. The children of God have eternal life, righteousness, holiness and righteous acts.

Baptism   Church membership   good works   your pet hope   charity

Leaves of Good Works

...... not of works, lest any man should boast.
Ephesians 2:9

TEST QUESTIONS ON MAN ON PAGE 189.

LESSON XVII

GOD TESTS MAN

Carefully avoid giving the impression that the way of salvation is different in different ages. Make it a point to impress upon the children the fact that there is no other way of salvation than through the death of Christ.

PERHAPS you can remember when you were very small and were not allowed to go outdoors without some older person, much less cross a street. Now you go to school alone. When you were little, you had to be fed. Of course now you take care of all such things yourself. Mother does not always treat you the same way, because you grow older and more able to do things for yourself. God has not always treated the people in the world exactly the same way either.

Of course God Himself does not change—"God is a Spirit, infinite, eternal and *unchangeable.*" He cannot change, or He would cease to be God. But that does not mean that He always deals with people in just the same way. His ways of doing things may change, though He does not. change. We are going to study some of those changes in our next few lessons on the various tests to which God has put man.

One thing, however, we must remember carefully. God never changes His way of saving people. Whether it is Adam and Eve, or Moses, or Peter, or Paul, all had to be saved by the death of Christ on the cross. "Neither is there salvation in any other, for there is none other name under Heaven, given among men, whereby we must be saved" (Acts 4:12). Isa. 53:6 in the Old Testament, written hundreds of years before Luke wrote Acts, says that God laid on Him, the Lord Jesus Christ, all our iniquities. When Adam and Eve were in the Garden of Eden, and sinned, God could not forgive their sin in any other way than by the death of Christ, which was to occur long years afterward. It was right there in the Garden that He gave them the promise of the coming Redeemer. The reason He did not banish them and send them to Hell forever, was because He knew Christ would come and die for their sins.

God changes His way of dealing with people because of a lesson He wishes to teach to all mankind. He wishes to show that "The heart is deceitful above all things, and desperately wicked" (Jer. 17:9). He wishes all to know that "There is none that doeth good, no, not one" (Psa. 14:3).

So He has put men to various tests, and in every one man has failed: This shows that without God men can do nothing. When God has finished giving these tests, no one will be able to think that there is any chance that men could have saved themselves. Under every possible condition they will have failed. Sometimes in school, after a test, you may think, "Well, if the teacher had asked different questions, or if I had not been tired, or if I had had more time, I could have passed." Men will never be able to say anything like that to God, for His seven great tests will prove that they could not pass, no matter what the test.

An age is a period of time during which God puts men under a certain test. He tells them the conditions, but invariably, after a few years, it is very clear that they have failed, and are doing wrong instead of right, in that test. Five such ages, or tests, have passed. We are living in the sixth, and there is one more to come. Of course those who believe in the Lord Jesus, in any test, are saved. It is those who will not believe who fail the test, showing that without God they can do nothing. Of course those who are saved are not trying to pass the test themselves, by their own power. They have the power of God working in them.

NOTEBOOK SUGGESTION: Make the following points clear.

1. An age is a time when God tests men in a certain way.
2. God never changes, though He changes the way He tests men.
3. The way of salvation is always the same, by the death of Christ, under every test.
4. The purpose of the tests is to show that man cannot be good without God.

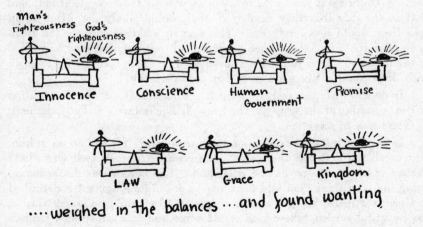

Man's righteousness   God's righteousness

Innocence   Conscience   Human Government   Promise

LAW   Grace   Kingdom

....weighed in the balances ... and found wanting

LESSON XVIII

GOD TESTS MAN

Try to lead the children to Christ as Saviour and Lord.
These are ideal lessons to teach the children from a diagram. Let them draw their own as they go (as described on the next page) and fit the events in. If there is a tendency to play with pencils while you are teaching, have them all lay them down except while they are being used.

THE first test that God gave to men was in the Garden of Eden. God created the first man, Adam, perfect, without any sin in his heart. He had no old nature, such as you and I have. Eve was also perfect. The Garden home must have been a very happy one, with no sin to disturb it.

God put man to the first test there in the Garden. He gave him just one commandment, and man was to keep that commandment perfectly. That sounds very easy, does it not? And yet man failed. The command was that he must not eat of the fruit of one of the trees in the Garden—the tree of the knowledge of good and evil. He might eat the fruit of all the other trees, but that one he must not taste. All went happily until Satan came in a beautiful form, to tempt the woman. He told her lies about God—saying that the reason He would not let them eat that fruit was because He knew it would make them as wise as He was. God had said that in the day that they disobeyed, they would surely die. But Satan said they would not surely die. The woman yielded, and ate the fruit. Soon after the man followed her example. In that moment they had failed in the first test. They showed that even with no sin in their hearts to begin with, they could not be good, and obey God perfectly.

In each one of these tests we want to see five things: 1. Man's condition at the beginning of the test. 2. The test. 3. The failure. 4. The judgment. 5. God's way of salvation.

In the first test man's condition was *innocence*. He had no sin in him. So we call the first test the test of innocence. The test itself was what? Perfect obedience to God's one command. The failure was disobedience, doing the very thing God told them not to do. The judgment is described in Genesis 3:16-19, 23. (Read and discuss.) Man could no longer stay in the beautiful garden, where God would come and talk with him. He had to go outside, where there were thorns and thistles and pain and sorrow and work that was hard and tiresome.

But the most important thing to see is the way of salvation. We can see it in two ways. The first is in Genesis 3:15, where God spoke to the devil. In that verse He spoke of the *seed of the woman*. Gal. 3:16 tells who the seed of Abraham is—Christ. The seed of the woman is the same. It means the Son of the woman. You know our Lord Jesus was not the son of any man, but He was the Son of a woman, Mary. God said to Satan that this Seed of the Woman would bruise his head, but that he, Satan, should bruise His heel. That is exactly what happened on the cross. Christ was hurt by the powers of Satan, but at the same moment, He crushed Satan forever. This verse, Gen. 3:15 is the first promise in the Bible of the coming Saviour. It was only through Him that Adam and Eve could be forgiven for their sin. The second way we see how they were saved is in the picture in Gen. 3:21. There God killed an animal, shedding its blood, and clothed guilty man and woman with the skins. This was a picture of how Christ would shed His blood in order that we might be forgiven. Salvation is always the same, you see—by the shed blood of the Saviour.

NOTEBOOK SUGGESTIONS: The following diagram is the first link of seven diagrams of the seven ages, or tests. Let each section fill one page, but show how the long horizontal line of the passage of time, will be continued for seven pages. Let the children choose a verse to write below "Way of Salvation."

The first test – INNOCENCE
      The demand – perfect Obedience

Man's condition was innocent

Failure through disobedience

Way of Salvation –
      The death of Christ represented by the slaying of a Lamb.

The Judgment was
1. Spiritual death
2. Driven from the garden.

LESSON XIX

GOD TESTS MAN

These lessons abound in practical points. Search out what applies to the daily life of the pupils, and apply right at the point where you are speaking of the subject. Such pointed lessons often remain lingering in the minds of the pupils.

AFTER Adam and Eve had sinned, they could never become innocent again. They had sin in their hearts, and they also had the knowledge of what was right and what was wrong. That is called *conscience*. Since that time every one has had a conscience—that which tells him whether he is doing right or wrong.

It was conscience that became the next test for men. They knew what was right; now would they do it? If they could pass this test they would show that they could be good of themselves, without God's help. But they did not. It was in this time that Cain killed Abel (Gen. 4). And by the end of this time men were so bad that God says all their thoughts were evil (Gen. 6:5). And finally, their wickedness was so incurable that God sent the flood to destroy all of them except one man, Noah, who had faith in Him. It was not that Noah was good, by his own power, but that he trusted God. He also offered sacrifices, which showed that he was trusting God for the sacrifice that would one day be offered on the cross—the Lamb of God that taketh away the sin of the world.

After the flood there was the third test. Man might have made the excuse that all should not be held responsible for Cain's being a murderer, and that if they had had government, they would have taken care of it in a righteous manner. So now God commanded men to govern each other, and to punish when men did wrong. In Gen. 9:6 He commanded that they should punish murder by death. That is the law of capital punishment, which is still observed. Because of this command of God for men to rule each other, we call this test the test of "human government." But they failed in this test, too, for men became more and more wicked and finally rebelled against God in building the tower of Babel. God had told them to replenish the earth, but they would not spread abroad on the earth, and instead wished to build a great tower and all live together. But God sent judgment again by changing their languages, so that they could not understand each other. (Story in Gen. 11.)

In the first three God has tested man as an individual, as a family and as a nation. He then set all other peoples aside and chose one man,

Abraham, to whom He gave special promises that He has partly fulfilled in Christ's first coming and will completely fulfill when the Lord comes again. Only one of the promises to Abraham had a condition attached to it, and that was the promise about blessing so long as Abraham stayed in the land. We call this fourth test, the age of promise. But Abraham did not stay in the land to which God sent him, and before long all his descendents had gone down to Egypt to live there. Then God had to send another judgment. All the people of Israel, as Abraham's descendents were called, became slaves in Egypt and for four hundred years they toiled and suffered there. All this was because of their failure to keep the one condition of staying in the land of promise.

Can you remember the first test? Man's condition was one of innocence. He had one command to obey, but he disobeyed, and died spiritually, and was cast out of the Garden. In the second test, men knew the difference between good and evil. That is called by what name? Conscience. But they did the wrong instead of the right, and the flood came. Then came another test, when men were to govern each other. But sin came again, and the judgment was the changing of their languages. Then came the fourth test of promise, with many blessings, but they left the place of blessing, and went to Egypt where there was nothing but sorrow for them.

All this time there was only one way of salvation. The sacrifices that were offered looked forward to the Redeemer Who would die to save them.

NOTEBOOK SUGGESTION: The following diagrams should take three pages, one for each age. Be sure the children choose a different verse to write beneath "Way of Salvation" in each chart.

The second test - Conscience

The demand - to do right and avoid evil

man knows right from wrong

Failure - Man does the wrong

Way of salvation -
The death of Christ represented by the slaying of a Lamb.

The Judgment was
The Flood.

The third test — Human Government

The demand — Man should govern for God

Man has power
to govern

Failure — Man tried to use his power against God by building Babel

Way of Salvation —
The death of Christ
represented by the
slaying of a Lamb.

the Judgment was
the changing of
languages

The fourth Test — Promise

The demand — to stay in the land of promise

Man has
received great
promises

Failure — He left the land

Way of Salvation —
The death of Christ
represented by the slaying
of a Lamb.

The Judgment
was slavery in
Egypt.

LESSON XX

GOD TESTS MAN

Try to lead the children to Christ as Saviour and Lord.
A review of the last lesson very briefly bringing out the salient points, will
make a fine introduction to this lesson, and will help to preserve the con-
tinuity.

THE people of Israel had a terrible time in Egypt, for they were ill-
treated for many years. But at last God sent a deliverer, Moses,
who led them out of Egypt and back to the land of promise.
On the way they camped at the foot of rugged Mt. Sinai, and there God
spoke to them, and gave them a new test, the test of law. Perhaps the
people might think, "Well, if we had a set of commands to tell exactly
what God wanted, we would not fail as we did under the other tests." God
gave them such a set of commands, the ten commandments, and a great
many other rules about everything they might do. When God spoke to
them they promised to do all that He said. But even before a month had
passed they had broken all the commands. (Tell the story of Exodus 32.)
And down through the years they continued to fail in this test, though it
lasted till the Lord Jesus died. God sent prophets to warn them, but still
they continued to fail in the test of the law. At last they killed the Lord
Jesus, and God judged the whole nation of Israel by letting their land be
conquered, Jerusalem burned and all the people scattered.

We read in the New Testament that the law was given by Moses, but
that grace and truth came by Jesus Christ (John 1:17). There was, of
course, law before Moses and there was grace and truth before Christ. But
law, *as a test,* began with Moses, and now grace, *as a test,* begins with
Christ. This is the one we are living in. It would seem to be the easiest
test of all, for the only thing God requires is that men should accept His
son, Jesus Christ, as the Saviour. Many have believed, and are saved, just
as in the other tests, many looked forward to the coming of the Saviour
and His sacrifices for them, and were saved. But many more refused to
believe. The real hard thing in the day in which we live is the test of
accepting God's Word that we can do absolutely nothing to save ourselves,
and that we must come to despise the works in which we have trusted,
and come to trust in the Saviour Who is the despised and rejected of men.
There are more people who do not believe in the Lord Jesus today than
there were a hundred years after Jesus died. How many of the boys and
girls in your school really love the Lord Jesus and believe in Him as Saviour?
Sad to say, very few. And in these days things are getting worse and worse,

for in many churches the ministers even preach that Jesus was not the Saviour, but just a good man! There will be a terrible judgment at the end of this test, too, after Jesus comes to take His own people out of the world to live in Heaven with Him. The great tribulation will come, and there will be a time of trouble worse than there has ever been. That will be the end of the sixth test.

The final test will last for a thousand years. Perhaps some people might say, "Well, the trouble all along has been the Devil. It wasn't our fault that we didn't pass the other tests for Satan tempted us." Of course that wouldn't be true anyway, for one never has to sin just because he is tempted. But the Lord gives His last test without even the Devil to tempt men. Jesus will come back to earth and set up His kingdom here, and the Devil will be chained for a thousand years, so that he can tempt no one. The world will be a wonderful place to live in then, for the Lord will not let any-one go on sinning. But even so, at the end of the thousand years when Satan is loosed for a little while, hundreds of thousands of people will follow him, and show that they hate the Lord Jesus Christ. What wicked hearts they must have, after having lived with Jesus here on earth for so long. At the end of this test, all the wicked will be judged by being sent away from God forever into torment.

Seven tests, and not one of them passed by men! How this shows us that we cannot do anything apart from God. Jesus said, "Without me ye can do nothing" (John 15:5). These seven tests prove that only those whom God saves are acceptable to Him, and can please Him. He must do everything for us, for we would always fail without Him.

NOTEBOOK SUGGESTIONS: To be added to the preceding ones, one on each page of note-
    book. Follow preceding directions.

Man
promises to keep   The 8th test _ Law
the commandments - the demand - To keep the commandments

        Failure - He broke the commandments

    Way of Salvation -
      the death of Christ
  represented by the slaying
  of a Lamb.
                                  the
                            Judgment was
                          being cast out of
                            their land.

The sixth test - Grace
The demand - to accept Christ as Saviour

Man is to
believe that
"All have sinned."

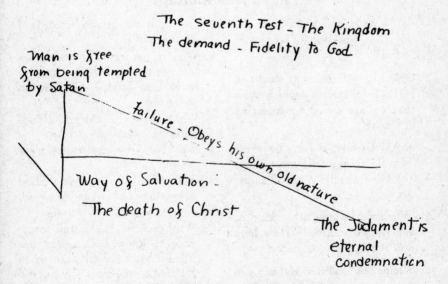

failure unbelief

Way of Salvation
The death of Christ who.
on the cross. fulfilled all the
Old Testament types.

The Judgment
will be "spiritual
death" and the
Great Tribulation,

The seventh Test - The Kingdom
The demand - Fidelity to God

Man is free
from being tempted
by Satan

failure - Obeys his own old nature

Way of Salvation :
The death of Christ

The Judgment is
eternal
condemnation

QUESTIONS ON THE SEVEN TESTS ON PAGE 189.

TEST QUESTIONS—COURSE FOUR

BELIEVERS AND UNBELIEVERS

1. How many kinds of people does God see in the world? What are they?
2. What does it mean to be *lost?*
3. Where were the believers' sins placed? Where are unbelievers' sins?
4. Is God the Father of all mankind? How do you know?
5. Did God the Father forsake the Lord Jesus on the cross? Why?
6. Is God angry with unbelievers?
7. (a) How can one go from Satan's family to God's family?
   (b) Write a poem of four lines telling how near you are to God.
8. Will believers be judged for their sins? Why?
9. Tell what you know about the home of believers, and the place to which unbelievers must go.
10. What are five differences between believers and unbelievers?

FULL ASSURANCE

1. Is "I hope so" a good answer to the question, "are you saved?" Why?
2. Give with references at least two verses from memory which show that we are saved by believing in Christ.
3. (a) Will God cast away believers who do things that are wrong?
   (b) Give definition of full assurance.
4. When we believe, what kind of life do we receive? How long will it last?
5. What does God demand of us in order that we reach Heaven?
6. How can we obtain what God demands of us?
7. What three kinds of people are there in the world? Do they differ in God's sight? Give reason for answer.
8. What answer would you give if someone asked you, "Are you saved?" Give reason for your answer.
9. Tell some of the wrong ideas people have about being saved, and why they are wrong.
10. Why does it give us full assurance to know that Christ finished the work of salvation when He died on the cross? What did He do for believers there?

STANDING AND STATE

1. What does *standing* mean?
2. What does *state* mean?
3. Draw a diagram to illustrate standing and state.
4. Name some of things which we receive as His heirs.
5. How could Paul say that the Corinthians were very good, when in the same letter he reproved them for many faults?
6. How do we receive the position of "sons of God?"

7. The Bible says that Christians are "glorified." How can this be when we still sin, and are so much unlike the Lord Jesus?
8. What does the Holy Spirit use to make our standing more like our state?
9. Whom shall we be like when our state becomes perfect?
10. When will our standing and state be just alike?

MAN

1. How was man different from anything else God created?
2. How do we know that evolution is not true?
3. Why did God create man?
4. What command did God give the first man and woman?
5. What was the first sin of man, and why was it sin?
6 In what way did the man and woman die when they sinned?

7. What effect did Adam's fall have on his descendants?
8. Do tiny babies have sin in their hearts? If so, why?
9. Tell about God's promise of a Redeemer to the man and woman in the Garden.
10. Tell about the agreements God made with Adam and with the Lord Jesus Christ.

GOD TESTS MAN

1. What is an age?
2. Does God ever change?
3. What is the way of salvation in every age?
4. Why did God give the seven tests to men?
5. Name the seven tests in their order.
6. Tell the story of one of the tests.
7. Did mankind pass any of the tests that are past? If so, which ones?

8. Will mankind pass the test of the Kingdom?
9. What will be the judgment at the end of the test that is going on now? What was the judgment at the end of the test of conscience?
10. What was the way of salvation in the test of law?
   (This is important. If they answer anything else than that it was by the death of Christ, you had better go back and teach that point all over again).